Sit Crooked and Speak Straight

Doing Business on the Arabian Peninsula

Stephen J. McGrane

Llumina
Press

Editorial assistance provided by Debra Christian of The Happy Guy Marketing.

ISBN: 978-1-62550-451-7

For Fasil

Table of Contents

Acknowledgments

I would like to thank all of my friends in Kuwait for their warmth and generosity during my years there: Sheikh Kalifa Al-Sabah, Mohanad Al-Murjan, Kalid Al-Saad, Adel Al-Yakoob, Anwar Dashdi, Bader Abrahim, Fasil Al-Saqer, Jamal Kasem, and Suhail Al-Zanki. They introduced me to the country and taught me about Arab hospitality. I would also like to thank Anwar Dashdi and Dr. Mohammed Al-Yakoob in Kuwait and Jamil Kasem and Moustafa Farouk in the UAE for taking the time and trouble to read the draft version of this book and providing me with valuable feedback to make it better. I would also like to thank Dr. Salam Al-Manasir in the UAE and Ahmed Al-Ahdal in Yemen for their friendship and support.

Chapter One

Introduction

The global environment of business has expanded to engulf a significant percentage of the American and European job markets. More than ever before, the everyday employee has a good chance of working – virtually or physically – with someone who was born, raised, or is employed in another country. No longer can we rely on dusty stereotypes or provincial attitudes in our professional lives. Now, in the 21st century, we must accept international associates as equals and even mentors as we learn to navigate the relatively new territory of global commerce.

Because the world is shrinking and we are forced to confront inaccurate perceptions of those who inhabit other cultures and workspace, it is necessary to set aside prejudices and misunderstandings to embrace diversity at our jobs and in our career paths. A generation or two ago, our parents and grandparents had little occasion to conduct business with people on the other side of the world. Overseas telephone calls took hours to connect, while letters required weeks to reach their distant destinations. Since international enterprises, somewhat limited as they were, operated through an intermediary or a small group of individuals, the other employees seldom met or became acquainted with associates on the other side of the world, separated by oceans, continents, language, and customs. It was easy to ignore differences and continue to operate in the same traditional ways. One could only hope that those in other lands eventually would "catch up" to our standard of business and be able to benefit from established connections and ongoing transactions.

But that method of doing business has altered dramatically. Several key events of the twentieth century have changed global commerce forever:

1. The progress of democracy.

Since the advent of the Industrial Age in the late eighteenth century, more nations, especially those once termed "third world" countries, have made strides toward developing democratic forms of government and officially joining the global market of free trade. Leaders of many countries throughout the world are eager to update business and industry to improve living conditions for their people and to contribute to the global community. However, don't expect democracy as we know it in the West to develop seamlessly elsewhere. Political change takes time, and people's notions of how their government should work and its role in their lives takes many forms. Westerners cannot expect that nations around the world will unanimously adopt our modus operandi. In fact, you can expect to find traditional views that find Western government and lifestyles to be distasteful and undesirable. No matter how archaic you may find some cultures, there will be men and women who hold to those values and fight against "invading" norms that we think are superior. So it is important to be patient and tolerant when experiencing alternative political systems and cultural mores that do not automatically fall into line with ours. Learning is as valuable as teaching when visiting other countries.

2. The evolution of women's rights.

When American women won the right to vote nearly one hundred years ago, their newfound public voice in the affairs of government and society made history and encouraged women in other parts of the world to push for similar freedoms. The result has been the growing involvement of women in politics, government, and business, as well as other significant fields that impact individuals and families everywhere, as evidenced by role models like Indira Gandhi, Benazir Bhutto, and Margaret Thatcher. That trend continues globally as women with restricted public visibility begin to enjoy greater rights and privileges that enable them to participate in public life. Conversely, those who prefer personal privacy or a sheltered family life continue to enjoy the freedom of these things without censure from outside forces. Women's rights, female employment, and related issues continue to draw attention and debate in many social structures around the globe.

3. The discovery of oil in the Middle East.

Sizable oil deposits found throughout the Middle East have led to dynamic changes in the global economy. Nations that previously had been relatively poor suddenly shot to instant wealth and power, with leaders of other countries clamoring to do business with them and gain a competitive edge over others with the same goal. Iran, Saudi Arabia, and other nations with similar oil deposits currently enjoy positions of prestige and authority while sometimes creating uneasiness for Western nations concerned about oil availability and cost. Oil is a brisk business throughout the civilized world, which is why countries with large reserves become key players in the economic management of distributing those reserves to other nations. The Middle East remains a global hot spot due to frequent disputes that impact oil sales among numerous countries that buy and sell this vital commodity.

4. The dawn of the Information Age.

For decades, computer wizardry has played a growing role in the way that we do business. From word processing to record management, computerized programs facilitated the paper load and sped up everyday work-related processes. The advent of communications technology, including email, voice mail, and high-speed Internet on the World Wide Web has revolutionized the ways in which people talk to each other and transmit information. Gone are the days of waiting for reports to arrive in the mail or emergency information to be sent by telegraph. Now, programs like Instant Messenger and cell phone texting allow us to communicate words and images to almost anyone (with the right equipment) in a matter of moments. Expanding communication borders means that we can talk to business associates around the globe in a matter of minutes. And when face-to-face meetings are required, we can travel there in hours. Business has never been better, faster, or easier on the face of this planet.

5. Increasing American and European presence in the Middle East.

Following the two world wars, a gradual, if uneasy, peace settled among countries that had fought each other during the first part of the twentieth century. While other war fronts like the Korean War and the Vietnam War continued to test Western strength and identify allied partners, it was not until the discovery and distribution of oil in the Middle East that new potential conflicts began to emerge. Initially, the U.S. and Britain established partnerships with countries like Iran and Saudi Arabia in order to keep a watchful eye on energy interests in the region. But with the 1979 Iran hostage crisis and the eventual Gulf War of the 1990s came the realization that peace would remain elusive for some time.

6. The growth of free trade.

Free trade has rapidly grown since World War II as trade barriers were decreased with the decline of nationalism and decreased transportation costs. Contributing to the globalization trend in the last twenty years has been the increase in international capital movements, increased manufacturing by developing countries, foreign outsourcing, digitization, and the Internet. The rise in globalization and the growth of free trade agreements has contributed to a 113% increase in U.S. exports to peninsula countries from 1997 to 2007.[1] Trade between peninsula countries and Europe and North America is expected to greatly increase in the coming years due to the further growth of free trade agreements. The U.S. currently has a free trade agreement (FTA) with Bahrain and an agreement with Oman is pending approval. There are also ongoing FTA negotiations with the United Arab Emirates (UAE). Additionally, the U.S. has a Trade and Investment Framework Agreement with Kuwait, Qatar, Saudi Arabia, and Yemen, with the goal of establishing a regional Middle East Free Trade Area (MEFTA) by 2012.

7. The surge of terrorist attacks.

Terrorist acts have increased dramatically since the 1970s and 1980s. Suicide bombers and guerilla militias have destroyed governments and assassinated key figures, all of which continues to play havoc with the global economy and East-West relations. The uncertainty of a terrorist group's success in destroying its target causes near-daily market fluctuations. Learning who can be trusted and how to avoid doing business with terrorists or the governments that support them are delicate issues that must be carefully explored in the ongoing quest for proactive negotiations.

Certainly, all aspects of global business have felt the impact of forces like these, and will continue to adapt with continuing changes in related areas. Lingering uncertainties will crystallize as more information comes into focus with respect to questions like these:

- Where will future communications evolution lead us?
- How will future travel impact business meetings and training plans?

- What role will women play in business as more countries undergo development?
- How will our world address the problem of shrinking oil reserves?
- What will be the outcome of Arab-Israeli peace negotiations?
- How and when will terrorism be brought under control?
- What is the future of free trade?

Although the answers to these questions continue to elude us now, they may materialize in the not-too-distant future, opening doors that we expected to remain locked forever.

In the Arabian Peninsula countries, business practices have evolved both rapidly and radically. Dazzling skyscrapers in glittering cities now attract visitors as much as romantic deserts and *wadis* in outlying areas. Investors are rushing to secure property and operate businesses in the lucrative, oil-rich Arabian Peninsula. Will their investments pay off? How will the Arab world respond to Western commercial infiltration? Will the West be influenced by Arab beliefs and culture?

The Arab states must be viewed as more than a business opportunity for Western entrepreneurs. Like the Yukon gold rush more than a century before, prospectors might find a different sort of treasure than those they now anticipate. If so, will they leave the Arabian Peninsula in better or worse shape than they found it? Will the West impart a positive or negative legacy – or none at all? What responsibilities must we accept for the privilege of doing business in Arab countries?

The peninsula region boasts a rich and illustrious history that is worthy of study in its own right. Moreover, the customs of the Arab people play a vital role in the way they conduct business. Their values, so different from those of Western nations, are worth considering and deserve appreciation. An astute businessperson who truly wants to leverage a win-win enterprise in the Arabian Peninsula can begin preparations for success by absorbing information about the social climate of this region in this book and putting it into practice during business negotiations with Arab hosts.

Whether you are planning a first business trip to the Arabian Peninsula States or have been there many times, a review of Arab culture and communication can help to facilitate your trip and enable you to fit in smoothly and successfully. Moreover, you can share this information with business associates who can benefit from tips to help them prepare for the adventure of doing business in the Arabian Peninsula.

Family members of business travelers should also plan for their visit by taking note of appropriate public behavior and rules of conduct, which can vary widely from one Arab country to another, although most share similar guidance from their shared Islamic faith and *shar'ia*.[2]

Casual visitors or tourists also need to know what to expect when traveling to or through this region of the world. Going unprepared can be time-consuming and costly; in some cases, it can lead to complications that can be difficult to untangle.

In planning your trip to the Arabian Peninsula, keep in mind that you will be meeting and working with other people who, in many respects, are much like you. They have family cares and business goals. They want to make a good impression and establish meaningful partnerships. They are eager to build a credible business standing in the global community.

Conducting business in a foreign culture can be frustrating and confusing. However, knowing something about how your counterparts approach business and social issues can relieve some of the uncertainty. With a little bit of time and preparation on your part, you can expect maximum enjoyment and satisfaction from your experience of doing business in the Arabian Peninsula and improve your business opportunities. You will see amazing new things and gain insight to an intelligent and experienced business mindset. Use this book as your introduction to the Arabs with whom you will conduct business.

Who Are the Arabs?

Business is booming on the Arabian Peninsula, and more Westerners than ever before are enjoying mutually beneficial professional relationships in the peninsula countries. The Arabian Peninsula, which is the focus of this book, encompasses seven Arab nations, with Saudi Arabia the largest. Others are Kuwait, Bahrain, Qatar, Oman, Yemen, and the UAE. Located between Iran and East Africa, and south of Iraq as well as Jordan, the peninsula beckons travelers from around the world.

In the western part of the peninsula, within Saudi Arabia, are Islam's holy cities of Medina and Mecca. The central region of the peninsula is largely desert and connected to the coastal towns by super highways filled with SUVs and Mercedes. The eastern coastlands comprise Emirates, with oil fields, sea trade, and agriculture.

Today colloquial dialects have replaced classical Arabic. These dialects differ so greatly that Arabs cannot easily understand each other nowadays. Because the language unifies the many tribes and regions of the peninsula, the use of variant dialects may chip away at Arab unity over time. Western travelers today should expect to encounter divergent accents and vocabularies, though many words and phrases are recognizable throughout the peninsula. It is a good idea to learn a few Arabic expressions for a particular area in order to make a favorable impression and to help you begin to make meaning from the language that others will be speaking around you.

The earliest European visitors to the region were the Portuguese during their infamous 15th century era of globalization and discovery. Vasco de Gama explored Oman's coast and the Strait of Hormuz in 1498. Today in Bahrain you can see a beautifully restored Portuguese fort from this period. By the early 1600s, the British established a branch of the East India Company in the Gulf region as a way station for travel to India. French and Dutch trading companies soon followed, though British forces had largely evicted these competitors by the mid-18th century. By the early 20th century, Ottoman Turks and Germany also manifested interest in the region from beyond the peninsula, while an internal uprising was led by Abdul Aziz bin Abdul Rahman Al-Saud. The Saudi conquests led to the formation of a state named Saudi Arabia. Factions within the peninsula have clashed with other factions as well as European powers.

Arabia, as the peninsula may be called, is the homeland of the Arab people and is the birthplace of Islam, one of the world's most widespread and fastest-growing religions. In the seventh century A.D., the Arabs, a Semitic people living in the desert of the Arabian Peninsula, began to spread Islam—and with it, Arab culture and language—across great distances to many regions. Islam also attracted merchants, adventurers, and traders who took the faith and culture with them to their own countries. Since then, the Arab population has diverged into the *Bedu* (Bedouins) and *Hadhar* (settlers), with most claiming tribal descent from one of the thirteen tribes of the Arabian Peninsula.[3] Following the Arab nationalism movement of the 1950s, the term

'Arab' began to be applied to all people who spoke the Arabic language. Today the Arab culture stretches from Morocco to Iraq and includes many dialects, ethnic groups, and customs. Because of these far-reaching distinctions, this book will limit its focus to the Arabian Peninsula, wherein the people and societies are more homogenous.

Distinctive Arab Culture

Culturally diverse, the Arab countries are supremely hospitable and welcoming to Western visitors who display suitable decorum and appropriate protocol. Although the culture can seem alien at first to Western visitors, the people and their customs can be easy to understand to those who apply themselves to learn something of their way of life. The essence of its "difference" deserves recognition for the valuable traits that have helped to preserve this way of life for hundreds and perhaps thousands of years.

Among Arabic people, collectivism takes precedence over individualism. A person will put the family, tribe, or country ahead of himself or herself. "Collectivist cultures are interdependent; as a result, the members work, play, live, and sleep in proximity to one another."[4] Group maintenance is a primary value. Emotions that counter the mood of the group are suppressed. Core values are honor, face (*wajh*), and hospitality.[5] These values preside over every meeting and relationship. It is important for Western visitors to learn the do's and don'ts of verbal and non-verbal communication in Arab countries. Although these will be covered later in the book, one example is to avoid sitting so that the sole of your foot faces another person, as this is considered inappropriate.

In the Arabian Peninsula countries, women and men lead different lives in many ways. The prevailing custom of modest dress means that men do not wear short pants or shirts that reveal the chest or back. Arab women may veil themselves in public in a variety of ways, from a simple head scarf to a complete head-to-toe body covering that lets them see through a small facial slit. Western women do not have to veil, but should wear skirts that fall below the knee, or alternatively, loose-fitting slacks. In Arab homes, the *majlis* or *diwaniyah* (sitting place or council) is the public room or area where men receive guests, a common, if not daily, occurrence. The *haram* (private place) is the area reserved for family use, and where women carry out domestic chores. Guests should avoid this part of the house unless specifically invited there.

Business is conducted very differently from how most companies operate in the West. Time is measured in slower and less compelling ways, with a more relaxed approach to schedules and appointments than is found in Europe and the U.S. A hurried attitude or glitzy presentation can create a bad impression. In some areas, women simply cannot conduct business, and they may need to cover their hair in public. For the most up-to-date customs and regulations, check government guidelines and the Web sites in Appendix E when planning your trip.

Who This Book Is for

Before doing business in the peninsula, it is important to learn about Arab culture, business culture, business etiquette, and negotiating techniques used.

Commercial, educational, and professional interests have blossomed under the careful tutelage of Arab-European/North American companies, corporations, and organizations. Business and industry have formed co-ops and teams that encourage members from Western and Arab nations to learn from and share information with each other. Tourists from all over the world visit the Arabian Peninsula, and some are employed there, which adds a rich cultural dimension to a Western traveler's experience. Likewise, entrepreneurs, government officials, and military service personnel can benefit from studying Arab culture. Anti-Western sentiment generally is not as pronounced in the Gulf region as it is in other Muslim nations. Although the British have made various treaties with the Arabian Peninsula states over many years' time, relations between East and West have maintained a cordial aspect that have not led the Arabs to suspect imperial interests or control issues, as has been the case elsewhere. Relations remain largely favorable for continued tourism and trade.

Cross-Cultural Training

Arabs and Muslims are becoming more numerable in Europe and North America via tourist, academic, and commercial avenues. Their effect on these societies is growing. With increasing media and political attention to nuclear proliferation, Middle Eastern politics, and the "war on terror," Westerners are developing a keen interest in the Arab world, its customs, traditions, political problems, and people. The more that Americans and Europeans learn about Arabs, the sooner they will abandon stereotyped impressions. With insight will come understanding, and what may seem confusing or complex now could become more clear and appreciable later, leading to enhanced relations and promising business prospects.

Thanks to the Internet, the world is rapidly shrinking. Instant chat has replaced transatlantic letters and the interminable wait for an overseas phone line. Teleconferencing is a growing medium for conducting long-distance business. Whether you are connecting to Arab associates via the Internet, by telephone, or in person, it is vital to grasp the context in which such communications take place in order to facilitate interactions and reach professional or personal goals. Verbal, nonverbal, and written language media need to be understood in ways that differ substantially from Western communication.

This book offers experience-based information and research to help Westerners understand Arab culture, communication, business attitudes, proper etiquette, negotiation, contracts, and social life. Readers can skip to specific chapters or passages for answers to their questions, or read the entire book for a broad-spectrum approach to culture appreciation. What to wear, do, and say will be explained, along with the most suitable ways of accomplishing these things. Also included are tips on what to avoid doing wrong.

Travelers to the Middle East sometimes view Arab culture as exotic and even abnormal when compared to a Western lifestyle. But those who carefully consider these seeming differences will notice similarities with Latin America and Mediterranean regions in terms of climate, terrain, food, and customs. Emotional and vibrant, Arabs are nonetheless bound by stringent rules. Westerners who explore Arabic culture and make an effort to be considerate while respecting these rules will find contact with Arabs to be a rewarding experience that will foster the growth of business and social networks to last a lifetime.

Doing business in peninsula states can be very different to conducting business elsewhere in the world. It may help to understand the rise of regional prosperity due to its abundance of oil, the social climate against which international commerce plays out, and the gradual and immediate changes that are occurring around the peninsula.

The discovery and development of oil as a natural resource made the Arab nations very wealthy by the 1970s. Among the oil-rich countries, Saudi Arabia is the main producer and a member of the Organization of Petroleum Exporting Countries (OPEC), the world's largest consortium of oil producers.[6] As other energy sources, such as solar, thermal, and natural gas, emerge, Arab oil revenues may decrease, but the global demand remains strong for now.

Whether you are a traveler-in-training, an experienced visitor to the Arabian Peninsula, a student about to embark on a college semester in the Middle East, a military serviceperson about to be deployed to that region, or a simple tourist in search of cultural enlightenment, this book offers a basic understanding of the cultural values and social norms that can make your trip meaningful and memorable. You can skip around to find special chapters of interest or read the entire book to absorb all the provided information that will help you to understand your Arab hosts and appreciate the world in which they live and work. This book is not a comprehensive list of everything you will need to know to do business in the peninsula but provides information for major areas.

Chapter Two

Arab Culture

When visiting a new culture for the first time, a practical traveler will want to understand the underpinnings of its society in order to communicate effectively within the cultural framework. All cultures operate on several principles that guide its members through daily life and periodic events. Visitors can benefit from understanding and utilizing these principles in order to negotiate potentially confusing and even frustrating differences while embracing commonalities that can build meaningful personal and business relationships.

Cultural Determinates

American and European cultural dimensions generally include individualism, egalitarianism, democracy, direct communication, low uncertainty avoidance, a short-term orientation which seeks immediate returns, and a future-oriented view of time that values planning and change.

In the Arabian Peninsula, cultural dimensions vary widely from those of Western cultures like the United States. Dr. Jehad Al-Omari (2003) describes four Arab cultural determinants that are useful in understanding Arab culture. They provide background for understanding cultural differences and can help a businessperson learn to communicate and transact business effectively while in the peninsula. These determinants can be found largely throughout the Middle East, but they enjoy special status on the peninsula.

1. Collectivism.

Collectivism may be defined as the organization of strong, solid groups whose values, opinions, and goals are considered more important than those of an individual. In contrast to the people of North America who continue to share values instilled by their ancestors who settled

Canada and the United States by relying on rugged individualism and personal effort, Arab culture is based on a shared existence that descends from a tribal mentality and continued extended family identity.

In Asian countries, collectivist societies are established by relationships more than the work itself. Shame is a greater motivator than guilt, while integration for the good of all supersedes individual rewards. Courtesy, humility, and hospitality are governing principles that guide business transactions to successful conclusions, as opposed to competition and aggressiveness in the West.

Teams and networks carry out the tasks associated with a process, and mediators resolve any resulting issues. Consensus-building is integral to the Arab business world and direct conflict or confrontations are avoided.

Comprehending the role of relationships is vital to doing business in Arab culture. Relationships need not be equal, as one might expect in a capitalistic society. For example, an Arab businessman might consult tribal relations, family connections, and business associates for help in addressing a dilemma or making a major corporate decision. Some Asian regions like India and Southeast Asia are matriarchal, while age is respected in most collectivist cultures. A Westerner might chomp at the bit while awaiting the opinion of an aged member whose views are sought by the negotiating parties.

Other attributes of collectivism to keep in mind include the following:

- Hidden power bases
- Hierarchical structures
- High personal disclosure
- Networking
- Saving face
- Slow negotiations
- Use of intermediaries[1]

2. High Power Distance.

"Power distance is the extent to which members of society within a country expect and accept that power is distributed unequally and that differences do exist according to status."[2] High power distance organizations are highly centralized, multilayered, and less democratic. While

Islam and tribal societies are traditionally low power distance, emphasizing equality, the reality is that organizations are hierarchical. The realities of hierarchy play a distinctive role with respect to authority in the realm of industry and business. Status-based differences technically operate in most societies, whether we openly acknowledge them or not. In Arab society, it is understood that some individuals wield more power than others because of their status, and this is generally accepted. A wide spectrum in pay differentials is also not unusual.

Hierarchy is manifested in several important ways throughout Arab business. The savvy Western traveler will do well to note these and prepare a visit accordingly:

- Distinctions between management and subordinates are clear-cut.
- Organizations are bureaucratic with people bound by the rules and reluctant to take initiative.
- Elderly persons are accorded great respect and should be greeted first.
- Men (rather than women) play key roles in business transactions.
- The "silent observer" may make more decisions than the speaker.
- A lack of transparency leads to rumors.

Western democracies that are unfamiliar with these practices may feel somewhat uncomfortable at first. But understanding their normalcy and predictability can help to ease tensions and promote productive meetings and transactions. It is important to identify the senior members of a business meeting and greet them first, followed by the others, in descending hierarchical order.

3. Polychronic Society.

The polychronic system involves multi-tasking at various levels of society. It "stress[es] involvement of people and completion of transactions rather than adherence to preset schedules. Appointments are not taken seriously and, as a consequence, are frequently broken."[3] Delays, interruptions, and postponements are common in the Arab business world, and Western visitors should be ready to practice patience and maintain focus.

Business may be conducted indirectly or directly against a backdrop of family affairs, frequent visitors, and competing interests. Arab businessmen may invite you to their homes on what appears to be a social context, and while that may be true, there also is the opportunity to foster personal relations that will impact business interactions that follow.

4. High-context Communication.

In a high-context culture situational communication is as vital as, or more so than, linguistic communication. Where, when, how, and why a person behaves and speaks – or remains silent – plays a major role in understanding what is going on during personal, social, or professional interactions. In high-context communication, most of the information is in the physical context or internalized in the person, rather than the explicit spoken part of the message. "In high-context situations or cultures, information is integrated from the environment, the context, the situation, and nonverbal cues that give the message meaning that is unavailable in the explicit verbal utterance."[4]

When communicating with people from a high-context culture, you must listen for hints and watch the body language for meaning of the message. Personal space, eye contact, physical contact, handshakes, and seating arrangements are all part of the message. If the message you are getting from the body language conflicts with the spoken message you are getting, body language should take precedence.

Some business considerations for high-context cultures are:

- Meetings approach issues in a holistic, circular fashion rather than linearly.
- Negotiations are slow and repetitive.
- Everything is negotiable.
- Negotiators are patient and persistent.
- Indirectness is a form of politeness. (Do not misinterpret this as being evasive.)
- People tend to avoid risk.

Communication Patterns

Within human communities is found a cultural speech code that is distinctive to location and identity. Just as inhabitants of certain regions enjoy similar meals, jobs, and fashions, so do they tend to adopt a related manner of speaking. Even intercultural groups centered on professions, hobbies, or interests share common connections in language and communication styles. Not only can we often recognize a person's ethnicity or race, barring other distinguishing characteristics, by the way he or she communicates, but we also can learn to understand the basic principles or "ground rules" associated with that communication style and become familiar with what to expect during discussions or negotiations, based on speakers' use of vocabulary, dialect, syntax, and pronunciation. In the Arab countries, this communication code can be described as a general attitude or cultural value called *musayra*.

Musayra

Musayra refers to the Arabic concept of accommodating others with the goal of building consensus and avoiding hostilities.[5] Building on the previously-noted values of honor, hospitality, and collectivism, *musayra* reflects a communication pattern that is indirect, respectful, polite, and non-aggressive. The goal is to make others feel comfortable, welcome, and valued through sensitive and low-key speech patterns.[6] This is achieved in four principal behaviors:

1. **Repetition.** Repetitive statements generally take the form of praise and compliments, which are important in a culture that strives to accommodate guests and its own members. Repetition also can be heard in debates as a form of persuasion, or influence, in lieu of Western-style argument.
2. **Indirectness.** Rather than directly contradicting a person with whom the speaker disagrees, he is more likely to take an indirect path that helps to save face and reiterate a courteous environment in which to discuss potentially challenging issues.
3. **Elaboration.** A comprehensive communication style provides opportunities for expansive expression and details. Dialogues of this type promote deeper, more meaningful relationships.
4. **Effectiveness.** An emotive speech style invites a more intrinsic level of engagement in professional or social dialogue that, like the other components of *musayra*, can lead to rich conversation and information exchanges.

Although the Arab world comprises geographically distinct areas and peoples, *musayra* can be noted in various aspects of each region. Travelers to the Arabian Peninsula need to be aware of the *musayra* code in communication patterns and understand its implications for business negotiations. Although Westerners may interpret this style of speech as representing uncertainty and passivity, and therefore think to press an advantage on these perceived weaknesses, that would be an inaccurate assessment. Rather, the astute Western visitor will perceive the *musayra* communication style as reflective of Arab culture overall and of his host's respect and accommodation, in particular. This observation should encourage Western guests to respond in similar fashion to reciprocate the gesture of accommodation.

Rhetorical eloquence is a common feature of Arab speech and should be recognized as such, rather than as a means of manipulation or deception. An Arab host might use lofty metaphors and exaggeration to make a point: "Your kindness is like a cool breeze from a tall mountain on a very warm day." While Westerners need not emulate this lyrical style, neither should they take it lightly nor reply humorously to statements like these, as they are meant to be sincere. Linguistic eloquence is an art form, one that Arab speakers have mastered for centuries. With minimal effort you can begin to understand and appreciate the roots of this timeless language and learn some basic expressions to facilitate communication.

The Arabic Language

Arabic is the official language of approximately twenty nations, is spoken by roughly 220 million people, and is the fourth most widely used language in the world, after English, Spanish, and Mandarin Chinese. Along with Hebrew and Amharic (Ethiopian), Arabic is one of the few Semitic tongues still spoken in modern times.[7] Since 2002, the demand for Arabic language classes in higher education in the U.S. has increased by more than 127%, far more than any other language.[8] Modern Standard Arabic and Colloquial Arabic are the two main forms of the spoken language currently in use; yet, dialects in various regions differ from each other in the same way as Spanish in Spain and South America, for example. With its naturally occurring rhythms and rhymes, Arabic is pleasant to hear and rich in vocabulary, as well as complex in syntax. Critical to the cultural importance of Arabic is the belief that God revealed the Qur'an in that language, adding reverence to its rich heritage as well as beauty in the formation of its script.

Assertion and exaggeration are common characteristics of spoken Arabic. Both represent cultural attributes and are necessary for clear and effective communication. The tendency to overemphasize an idea and its meaning may come down from an earlier point in history when bartering was an operative necessity in the export and import business derived from caravan and seaport trade. Active participation in the marketplace of commodities at the crossroad of cultures required Arabs to speak loudly and emphatically to compete for potential customers' interest.

Emphatic speech is another tendency among Arab speakers. Westerners may get the impression that an Arab person is being over-dramatic in outlining his views or preferences. Exaggeration is a common practice that is expected and understood within the culture. Conversely, Westerners who simply state what they mean in direct fashion may find that they are not taken seriously or may be perceived as saying "yes" when they really mean "no." Travelers to the Arabian Peninsula states may find it helpful to listen to native speakers before engaging in communication on their own.

An example of how the Arabic language potentially reflects commercial activity and has infiltrated Western vocabulary is the word *risk*. Given that taking a risk is an admirable business trait nowadays, it is interesting to note the legend that risk-taking is an Arab invention. European traders of the Middle Ages allegedly adopted the word *risk* from adventurous Arab traders who sailed abroad in search of *rizq* (Arabic for "a living" or "fortune").

Written Communication

Planning a visit, arranging meetings, and conducting business often are managed in large part through written communication, which for Western businesspersons means English. Although many Arabs speak excellent English and even may have received a Western education, do not presume that those who speak good English likewise can read and write English well. By following a few basic rules for written communication, you can greatly improve the odds of having your materials read and understood.

- Avoid slang. Although your Arab hosts may use it in speech, there is no certainty they can understand it in written form. For business documents, slang is inappropriate in either Western or Arab culture.
- Use simple sentences. Avoid compound or complex sentences to ensure that each sentence relays one main idea that is easily grasped.
- Check your writing for spelling and grammar errors.
- Don't be afraid to display a conservative human side by using mild humor, which helps to build all-important relationships. Arabs enjoy upbeat humor, like a business-related cartoon that relays a key point, which can be used on a fax cover sheet or other peripheral materials.[9]
- Do not use figures of speech or off-color references that can be offensive and/or misunderstood.

The Arabic language, like the culture it represents, is values-based. Expect to find in documents or correspondence addressed to you statements that utilize phrases like *kind* and *honor*.[10] You may want to consider using similar phrasing in your documents.

While preparing materials for your business meetings in Arabian Peninsula countries, use the best quality of paper and ink as well as folders, binders, etc. Include an Executive Summary, preferably in Arabic, with longer documents. Many Arabs can understand English, but some may have difficulty reading it.

Your business cards should be printed in English on one side and in Arabic on the other. Ask a competent translator to check the Arab version for accuracy.

Because Arabic is considered a holy language (used to transmit divine knowledge to the Prophet for the Qur'an), English should not be mixed with Arabic on the same page.[11] Some Arab businessmen will accept a two-column document of English and Arabic side by side. In any case, bring your choice of hired translator along on the visit to the peninsula, and if it becomes necessary to translate documents into Arabic, provide a reasonable amount of time for this to be done. Quality and accuracy are very important to the success of your business trip.

Oral Communication
Linguistic Symbols

More than Westerners, Arabs use words as symbols rather than as absolute meanings in their own right. This is due in part to the philosophical approach to culture that overlaps into the linguistic realm, rendering Arabic a fluid and flexible language. Western visitors who do not know Arabic may well be hard pressed to correctly translate Arabic expressions or clearly understand what an Arab speaker is trying to convey in certain English statements. For that reason, it is a good idea to hire a reliable interpreter who can help to glean comprehensive meaning from spoken communication. Because the Arabic mind is expansive, fitting a thought to a word is more of a token gesture than an absolute idea. Overemphasis and assertiveness can overwhelm a Westerner who is unfamiliar with the linguistic tendencies of his Arab host.[12] While this is a normal way of making a logical point in Arab culture, a Westerner may feel perplexed about the speaker's "bottom line." Conversely, when a Westerner simply states his position without exaggeration or emphasis, an Arab listener may feel the speaker is making a tenuous statement. For example, responding with a simple *no* may encourage an Arab counterpart to press forward rather than give up.

It is a good idea to learn a few Arabic words and expressions, not because they are needed, since many Arab businessmen already know English, but because this language skill makes a good impression on your hosts.

Eloquent speech is regarded as the hallmark of a refined and educated person in the Middle East, although in the West, a practical and simple linguistic style is preferred. In the Arab nations, context should guide a foreigner's interpretation of how something is said, as well as what is said. Many kinds of florid expressions can be heard in an Arab's speech that may startle, distract, upset, or confuse a Western listener, such as:

- Boasts
- Threats
- Slogans
- Extreme promises
- Stories

Even home-based entertainment makes use of jokes, word games, anecdotes, and verbal competitions in ways that are not often seen in European or American societies. The Arabic language is handsomely scripted and beautifully spoken; speakers take great pride in its unique features and enduring popularity.

Arab speakers make full use of their vocal range and body language (especially hand gestures) to get their point across. Loud voices imply passion, not anger. Sometimes it is difficult to know if two people are conversing or arguing – another example of the need to understand the high-context nature of Arabic culture.

The Islamic faith has made inroads into everyday speech, with an obvious example being that of *inshallah*, "if God wills it." Visitors to the peninsula or any Arab nation will hear this statement made innumerable times each day by people from every walk of life. Yet, the meaning of this expression can vary from one speaker to another, based on context, intonation, and other factors. A man I knew in a peninsula country once saw a man yelling at and hitting his foreign driver. The local was telling the driver to pick him up at a certain time and place. The driver was responding by saying "I will be there, *inshallah*." Each time the driver said that, the man told him to say he would be there without saying *inshalla*, and hit him again. My friend knew what was going on. The driver was religious so he could not talk about an event in the future without mentioning God's will, since only God can determine what will happen in the future. The local understood it to mean that he was not going to be there because he would not say it without saying *inshalla*. When my friend explained to the local man that the driver was religious and he would be there – only God could prevent him from it – then everything was fine.

This story is a good example of an attribution error. Attribution is the process by which we interpret communication based on our own culture. Attribution errors occur in cross-culture communication when we apply our own cultural interpretations to another culture, thereby misjudging the meaning of a nonverbal message. The problem here was not the hitting. It is common for a superior to hit a junior to show he means what he says; remember body language means more that the words. (A junior would never hit a senior. Also, you as a foreigner should not hit anyone to show you are serious; it won't work.) Although both men were the same religion and spoke Arabic, they were from different cultures. Because of this, they made an attribution error. Each interpreted the word according to his own culture rather than the context. It also shows how the word *inshallah* can have different meanings, and that context must be considered for proper interpretation. Because it is a high-context culture, more weight should be given to the context or situation than to the actual words. With time, you will develop a practiced ear that can help you decipher hidden and stated messages.[13]

Exaggeration

Westerners tend to view with suspicion those who use exaggerated speech. But Arabs exaggerate to have a strong impact on listeners. Numbers may be rounded up, details can be heightened, or a situation made to sound better or worse than it usually is (better, mostly) for the purpose of getting a point across. No harm is intended usually, and listeners should evaluate the information for accuracy if it is important; otherwise, hyperbolic comments and descriptions should be taken with a grain of salt and left unchallenged.

Euphemisms

Most, if not all, languages make use of euphemism, that is, saying negative things in positive ways. Ways of doing this include using generic rather than harsh words and concepts, specifically with regard to illness, suffering, and death. You may be told that an older family member won't be coming to your host's home to visit today because he is preoccupied or unavailable. Only later will you learn that the elderly person has a serious disease or has been incapacitated. The intention behind such statements is not to mislead, but rather to avoid upsetting listeners or to play down the seriousness of a difficult situation.

Words vs. Deeds

Due to the Arabic habit of utilizing oral and written language as an art form, communication can appear contrived, elaborate, flattering, threatening, or deceptive. But the actual intent of many speakers is to create word pictures with language that help to convey emotions, ideas, and abstract thinking. Thus, language may seem rather far removed from the practical goal at hand. However, as in studying artwork, it is important to notice the basic structure, theme, and purpose to grasp the full meaning of whatever is being said.

Language is not always absolute in expression or meaning. For example, you may expect another member of your host's business firm to join your meeting that is in progress. Asking your host when to expect the new arrival, you could be told, "He's coming; he'll be here soon." In fact, the expected guest may arrive quite late or not at all, as your host responded to your question with a general notion that the guest in question is expected and may very well show up as planned, or he might not. If you don't receive specific details, don't take literally everything that is said.

Compliments

Compliments from Arab speakers can be lavish and extreme, in keeping with the flourishes and arches of the speaker's rhetorical skill. You may receive praise that is factually inaccurate referring to your physical appearance, character, social standing, or economic status. These compliments are intended to make guests feel welcome and accepted by Arab hosts and friends.

Silence

Many Westerners are uncomfortable with prolonged periods of silence when in conference with one or several business associates. Going without speaking for twenty seconds or more can create sweaty palms and racing hearts. Constantly surrounded by noise in our professional and personal lives, it can be difficult to reclaim silence as an enjoyable state, especially in company with others.

In the Arab world, however, silence is comfortable and welcome. A group of businessmen who have met to discuss a proposal or consider an offer may enjoy a spirited exchange for a time. Then it is not uncommon for them to switch gears and tell stories or trade gossip, after which they simply fall silent, as though mentally regurgitating all that has transpired, or taking a "timeout" from discussions to simply enjoy the quiet air that now permeates the room, perhaps while enjoying coffee or tea.

Do not be alarmed if this silence descends on your business meeting. It may signal a thinking phase, a rest period, or a transition between verbal activities. Note the expressions and manner of those in attendance and take your cue accordingly.

How to Say "No"

According to an Arab proverb, "no answer is an answer." Arabs are a non-confrontational people. They feel it is important to avoid conflict and to save face if someone should be accused of wrongdoing. Criticisms and accusations are reserved for private meetings between individuals. Honor and shame are two polar forces that guide much of the social interaction in Arab culture. Therefore, a negative response is given indirectly or not at all in order to be polite and prevent embarrassment.

It is impolite to say *no* directly in response to someone's question or request, although Westerners are accustomed to doing so in business and pleasure situations. Moreover, the speaker who does so may take the risk of being misunderstood. A simple *no* in Arab culture is considered a "soft" response that invites continued negotiations. Because overemphasis and exaggeration are traditional communication styles within the language, these tendencies are expected in business as well as personal exchanges. It is important to be clear and emphatic when stressing a point, especially one based on "no," such as rejection, inability, or insufficiency.

Uncomfortable with open dissension and arguments, many Arabs will appear to agree with a proposal, but then give hints that they do not agree at all. An astute communicator will watch for signs like the following within the high-context culture of business negotiations as possible "no" responses:

- A "soft" *no* – spoken once in a normal or low voice.
- A *yes* response followed by hesitation.
- A stalling or postponement tactic to avoid a negative response.

Be aware of several factors that may help you to interpret what the speaker is actually saying. These include repetition (or lack of), rationale, pauses, and related factors. Negative factors or conflicts are usually avoided in an open meeting, and they may need to be approached gradually or in a more private venue.

If you send someone an email asking a question and he does not reply to the email, you can assume the answer is no. You may call to confirm he got the email, but if the recipient says he got the email, you should not press the issue and force the person to say *no*.

To more quickly discern positive or *yes* answers from *no* answers, evaluate body language, context, and language cues. Because Arabs dislike saying *no*, they may seem to exhibit ongoing interest in your business, albeit in more of a casual vein, until you realize a firm commitment is not forthcoming, and then give up and go home. Your Arab hosts have not rejected your business proposal. They simply let it ride until you chose to leave, or try another tack later.

Once I was recommending to an importer friend of mine in an Arab country that he should consider being the agent for a new product that had just come out in the U.S. The company was looking for a distributer in the Middle East, but my friend would have to act fast to get the deal. His reply was that it sounded like a good idea, and we would discuss it next time I visited. Since he knew I would not be there for a year, and by then it probably would be too late, I knew he was not interested, but was avoiding saying it so as to not offend me. I therefore dropped the subject. (It is also possible that he did not want to commit because we did not know each other as well as I thought. This will be discussed further in Chapter Three.)

Vocal Signals

Many Arabs speak in a tone of voice that is louder than the average Westerner's. To Americans and Europeans, it may sound as though an Arab is excited or irritated, when in fact he is speaking in a normal tone for his language. Volume may increase during key discussions or debate sessions. The tone may sound emotional, although little emotion typically is introduced in business discussions.

Pitch is important, as it can represent a speaker's level of personal investment in the conversation, his or her emotional state, and the person's perspective on the issue at hand. Taken into account with other contextual factors, pitch can help a Westerner decipher the speaker's attitude toward the topic.

Nonverbal Communication

Because the Arabian Peninsula countries are high-context societies, nonverbal communication plays a vital role in assisting Westerners to fully understand a speaker's message. Language, of course, is the primary means of communication, but in Arab countries, body language adds layers of extra meaning that need to be translated, along with spoken words. Here are some of the most common examples of Arab non-verbal communication to watch for:

- A brief smile may indicate politeness rather than agreement in the Arab world.
- Head nodding (up and down) suggests agreement.
- Lifting the head up and rising the eyebrows or moving the chin back and clicking the tongue means "no" or "what you say is false."
- Touching the side of the nose, placing a hand on the head, or touching the side of an eye means yes.
- Placing the right hand on the heart after a handshake means the greeting came from the heart and is sincere.
- Holding the right hand out with palm down and fingers together and making a scooping motion toward the body means come here. (Beckoning with one finger is offensive.)
- Closing the hand halfway with palm up means give it to me.
- Holding the hand out with palm down and then twisting it up means "why."
- Leaning forward while speaking is a sign of warmth, while leaning back is a sign that you want to put distance between you and your counterpart.
- Pointing is not considered rude.
- Looking away too frequently is a sign of disrespect or evasiveness, looking down means embarrassment or subservience, and looking up means arrogant or condescending.
- Standing close to a person of the same sex is a sign of warmth and trust.
- Holding the tips of the fingers and thumb together and moving the hand up and down means "patience."
- Pulling the point of your chin means "shame."

The following anecdote will illustrate the uncertainty of understanding meta-communication in Arab culture. A few years ago, I was sitting in on a meeting in a peninsula country to negotiate a deal. There were five attendees from each party sitting on each side of the table with the senior man of each in the center. The meeting started out slowly, but soon voices started to rise. After a few more minutes, everyone was standing and shouting, shaking fists and throwing papers. I was sure there was going to be a fight and was watching the door, planning my escape. The senior man on one side then picked up a glass of water and threw the water in the face of the senior man from the other side. I was sure this was the end. But everyone then started to laugh and sat down. Things seemed to be back to normal and a few minutes later the meeting was over. Everyone left smiling, arm-in-arm. On the way out, trying to make sense of what just happened, I asked someone if the negotiations had broken down, or if the deal was off. He said "no," just the opposite, they had reached an agreement and everything was fine.

This story highlights Arab communications patterns that a Westerner can learn to recognize with the help of cross-cultural training before taking the trip. Gestures, emotions, and volume are normal ways to show sincerity; they do not always mean the speakers are angry. You must consider the situational context to evaluate the speaker's frame of mind.

Private vs. Public Courtesy

Cultivating acquaintances and friendships in Arab countries can help to facilitate business dealings and personal travel. Friends receive different, and usually better, treatment than strangers.

People that are known or received as guests can expect to receive courteous, truthful, generous, and thoughtful assistance anytime. Hosts go out of their way to make every guest feel welcome and valued, beginning with a warm greeting, proceeding to guest comforts, and continuing with open and accepting communication. Personal treatment is gracious and hard to exceed in other cultures.

But in public when you join the throng of strangers going about town or traveling around the area, you become subject to crowding, pushing, shoving, and overpricing. It is natural to feel frustrated and unappreciated, or perhaps even taken advantage of. It is important to stay calm and remain polite, even if you feel others do not treat you in the same manner. Causing an argument or making a scene will only make matters worse. Keep in mind that such treatment is part of the culture and is not meant to be insulting.

Social Standing

Three main people groups inhabit the peninsula: Bedouin nomads or semi-nomadic peoples with herds of camels, sheep, and goats; farmers and agriculturalists; and city dwellers. Bedouins are viewed with honor as the original settlers of the land from whom everyone else has descended. Due to extreme climate and terrain conditions, nomads cultivated wide-ranging friendships and partnerships with property owners who let them use pasturelands and wells for their herds. Consequently, networking and teambuilding became a way of life, and these practices are still valued today. Members of the nomadic groups held closely to their lineage as a means of identification and formed strategic liaisons. The tribal leaders, called *shaykhs*, are chosen based on their proven courage, insight, and connections.

The stationary farmers follow a similar form of local rule by choosing a leader with demonstrated skills from the tribal elders. Lineage plays a strong role in determining who is eligible to rule. Connections to nearby tribes or villages may lead to a man being chosen as *shaykh* of his territory, along with the ability to communicate with government and royal authorities on behalf of his tribe or village's interests.

City and town leaders are chosen by tribal tradition and family role by consensus of tribal representatives. Headship may be a birthright if the current candidate has appropriate credentials along with the town's trust to hold a position of leadership. Farming regions tend to avoid or distrust interaction with foreigners.

The family is the primary social institution. As mentioned previously, Arabs take pride in their common descent from the Bedouins generally, and from a particular tribe, specifically. Social rank and occupation often stem from these identifications and positions.

Within the business world of companies and organizations, family bonds carry greater weight than personal skills or professional qualifications. It is common to find several male relatives employed within the same organization at varying levels of status and responsibility; nepotism is common because leaders tend to trust family members over strangers. It is helpful to remember that the good of the group is more important than individual advancement. The oil-related income of the 1970s attracted nomads who sought to take advantage of the unexpected opportunities to adopt an urban lifestyle and obtain business or government employment. Most people sense a form of kinship among the local inhabitants of their region.

Arabians do not see society as a vast, impersonal mass of people containing a few individuals whom they will meet at various times in their lives and with whom they will form business or personal relationships. Rather, their world is made up of a web of communities, tribes and families – some they know personally, but all they know of.[14]

The lower layer of the social strata consists of Bedouins who sold their animals and settled in populated areas only to find they had no work skills that paralleled their former high social ranking. Thus, they were forced to take menial jobs and assume a lesser position in society or remain unemployed while waiting for work they consider suitable for their skills. Within this social group are included foreign workers who perform labor.

The Meaning of Time

Businesspeople in the United States and Europe tend to follow their schedules closely, and expect others to do the same. They do not like to be kept waiting or have appointments postponed at the last minute. No-show appointments are even more irritating, with some professionals billing the missed appointment to the client's account.

Time is money to Westerners. Consequently, many businesspeople handle time like money, parceling it out frugally, guarding it zealously, and applying it only where needed at the moment. Frivoling time away is not a popular pastime in the business world.

However, in the Middle East, and particularly for Arabs, this is not the case. Time is a vast resource that can be hoarded, used as desired, or even spent recklessly on occasion. Since Arab culture is polychronic, with multiple demands competing for attention at any given moment, odds are that business may fall lower on the totem pole than other interests, such as family, relationships, and pressing professional matters. With a history of desert life and sea voyages, measured time held little significance. With the Islamic faith a central pillar of society, the call to prayer became a daily milestone of passing hours.[15] Being diverted from a business meeting by a relative's urgent request or an immediate travel issue is perfectly natural to many Arabs who do business with those outside their countries. The society at large understands that leading businessmen may have to travel at a moment's notice with a senior official who must leave the country unexpectedly or convene a vital council on some pressing affair. Neglecting to cancel a missed business appointment and reschedule another with representatives of a Western firm may convey a sense of non-involvement, but the reality of the situation is that an Arab businessman realizes he has plenty of time to conduct his business affairs upon his return, in priority order.

Arabs tend to follow their gut feeling or a particular emotion when addressing key subjects related to business, rather than pay homage to a preset agenda or makeshift list of items to be covered at the meeting. Difficult topics or challenging problems should be addressed at the right moment, when one feels it is the best time to do so, rather than obey the clock in such matters.

This brutally clashes with the Western notion of hurry-up-and-make-the-deal while following a tight schedule. Often, an American or European businessman arrives in one of the peninsula countries with an itinerary and an agenda. If he is familiar with Arab business culture, he would have asked his secretary to confirm the details of his visit beginning at least two weeks before and intermittently up to the day of the scheduled visit. Even then, plans can change abruptly, so it's best to have a back-up plan. Moreover, it is unwise to become impatient or display irritation when an appointment is neglected, forgotten, or cancelled. You will get further by being a good sport and rescheduling the missed meeting. One expert suggests a ratio of 95% waiting time and 5% intense activity – sometimes against extreme odds or nonsensical deadlines.[16]

While it's true that younger Arabs, many of whom have been educated in the West, are more time-conscious than their fathers and grandfathers, an occidental who will be traveling to the peninsula to do business should be prepared to deal with the time factor. Because an increasing number of Arab businessmen are starting to keep time in the Western manner, always plan your trip with the goal of conducting business on a schedule, but remain flexible in the event of last-minute changes, delays, and cancellations. Expect to hear from time to time *inshallah* – if God wills it. Only He controls the future and knows what tomorrow will bring.

Personal Values

In Arab culture, personal and business values often overlap. Personal friendships can lead to business partnerships. In fact, it is difficult to conduct business in Arab countries until a mutually beneficial friendship has been established. A handshake carries more weight than a contract, so it is important to build a business relationship upon merits like trust, respect, and honor. Good character is admired as much as, or more than, financial acumen. Saving face, offering hospitality, and protecting honor are perhaps the most cherished values.

Proving friendship through a series of small but important actions can lay the groundwork for a more substantial business relationship. One way to do this is become familiar with Arab business protocol (to be discussed in greater detail later). Another way is to demonstrate respect for Islam, which to a great extent orders the schedule through the five daily prayers, weekends, and various fasting and feasting holy days.

Humility is greatly valued by Arabs, as self-aggrandizement is viewed as rude and crass. It is wise to use quality technology but best to avoid a glitzy presentation in favor of a simpler demonstration that will make your point without annoying your hosts.

Generosity, family commitment, and personal convictions without being over-assertive can help to create a positive image that will serve you well in the peninsula.

Personal Customs

The more time you spend in the Arabian Peninsula countries, the more comfortable you will become with social and business protocol and culture. Here are a few rules to keep in mind regarding Arab personal customs to help start you out:

- Avoid excessively admiring someone's possession, as he or she will feel compelled to give it to you.
- If your Arab host gives you a gift, or you present one to him, it should not be opened in the presence of the giver.
- When offered coffee or tea during a visit, it is good manners to accept at least one cup. You will be offered several rounds, so

place your palm over the cup or shake it when you do not want more.

- When an Arab host invites you to dinner, he expects to pay for your meal.
- When an Arab woman marries, she does not change her name.
- Kissing one or both cheeks in greeting is customary between family members or friends of the same sex.
- Handshaking with introductions is normal between men. However, do not expect to shake an Arab woman's hand unless she is somewhat Westernized and/or offers her hand first.
- Handshakes can last a long time and men may remain holding hands after the shake. Etiquette dictates that you not withdraw your hand until the other person withdraws his.
- Holding hands in public is common between Arab men, but not between Arab women or an Arab male and female couple. Females may link arms in public on occasion.
- Western male-female couples should avoid public kissing or embracing, as this is illegal according to Islamic law, subjecting them, if reported, to possible arrest in some countries.
- Use the right hand for greetings and handling food, as the left hand is customarily considered the hygiene hand.
- Modest dress for both men and women is required under Islamic law in Arabian Peninsula countries. Men should avoid exposing any part of the torso or leg, although knee-length shorts may be acceptable for certain sports events or special occasions. Women should wear loose-fitting slacks or skirts that are knee-length or longer, as well as tops with sleeves that reach at least the elbow and do not expose neck, chest, or back areas of flesh. Like men, women should not wear clothing that reveals any part of the torso. Failure to observe this mandate can lead to possible arrest, or in more liberal Arab countries, the observation that the Westerners in question have little knowledge of or respect for Arab customs, and perhaps even poor taste.
- The soles of the feet should not be turned toward an Arab person, as this indicates disrespect. Be careful about sitting with one or both legs crossed in such a way as to expose the sole of your foot to an Arab person in the room. It makes no difference whether

you are barefoot or wearing shoes. In general, it is best not to cross your legs while in the presence of an Arab, but if you do, take care not to show the bottom of your foot to anyone present.

- Hand usage and gestures are very important.
- Making the Western "okay" sign is also offensive, as it represents the "evil eye" in Arab culture.
- When seated in a circle, be sure that you have not turned your back to another person (for example, if someone is sitting just behind you), as this is considered disrespectful.
- Slouching while sitting is acceptable. According to an Arab proverb, you should "sit crooked and speak straight."
- Leaning toward someone to whom you are speaking is viewed as friendly, while leaning away suggests aloofness.
- When joining a council of businessmen or elders, do not take the highest-ranking seat to the right of the senior member, unless you are invited to do so.
- Follow the lead of your hosts when greeting new arrivals or saying good-bye to departing guests.
- Standing is essential during introductions, even for female Westerners who are not expected to stand in their own countries.
- Proximity while standing reflects the nature of a relationship, i.e., someone standing close to you (less than three feet) feels you are trustworthy. Maintaining a physical distance of more than a few feet suggests coolness.
- Greetings and departures may involve handshakes, hugs, or even light kisses on either cheek between two acquaintances of the same gender.
- Do not openly criticize Arabs or anything connected with them; deal with concerns privately and one-to-one.
- Do not indulge in profanity or coarse joking.
- Do not lightly introduce topics of religion, history, or politics.
- Do not speak of or to Arab women or women generally.
- Do not speak loudly or laugh hard in public; be self-contained.
- It is polite to visit someone you know in the hospital, where you will be greeted courteously by the acquaintance's family and perhaps offered tea or chocolates.

- You can wish a couple well on the birth of a child, and you can express condolences on the news of a tragedy or accident.
- Arabs do not say "please" and "thank you" as frequently as Westerners do because they are just words and do not end your obligation for a favor or service. Deeds are more important than words so favors and services are expected to be returned in kind. They are aware Westerners will consider it rude if these words are not used and will try to use them but do not be offended if you don't hear them every time.
- Learn the customary Arabic expressions to make your sentiment genuine and earn your Arab friends' respect and admiration.

While these rules may seem cursory and insignificant to a Westerner, they carry great weight in Arab culture. Following them may help to open doors to a successful business venture. Ignoring customs like these can have the opposite effect.

When in doubt about how to behave in various social and professional contexts, check with your agent, prior company representatives, or various texts on bridging cultural differences. You also can follow your host's lead if you find yourself in new territory. Arab people are very gracious toward their guests and will go out of their way to make them feel comfortable.

Like its unique and challenging geographical terrain, Arab culture offers surprising twists and turns that can leave a visitor feeling a little lost. An important principle to keep in mind is the value of personal relationships. Within families and tribes as well as among friends and even professional associates, personal connections built on trust are the cornerstone of establishing a meaningful presence in the region. Commercial success grows out of interpersonal relationships. The following chapters will explore additional facets of doing business in the peninsula states.

Chapter Three

Business Culture

Working in Peninsula Countries

B efore entering the Arabian Peninsula market you should analyze several business issues. These include business regulations, legal environment, tax laws, accounting methods, import/export regulations, labor regulations, foreign capital regulations, and exchange controls. Each country has different regulations on these issues so you should become familiar with them before you choose the market you want to enter. For example, there are differences in the amount of foreign ownership a business may have, some countries have regulations on the hiring of local manpower, and some countries have restrictions on who can trade in the local market. The World Bank Group has an excellent Web site that compares regulations and ease of going business (See Appendix E). Knowledge of the countries and their business culture and good market intelligence is essential for success.

Market Intelligence

Because many governments do not publish much business information it can be difficult to get the information you need to make decisions. Therefore, there are many rumors in the business community about what is going on. You should shift through these rumors and confirm what you hear with at least three sources before you believe it to be true. You should also of course have a system for obtaining market intelligence, which you can use to confirm rumors. This can be done with frequent travel to the region, publications, and maintaining a liaison with agents or government employees. These contacts will help to keep you informed about government plans and changes in the market (See Appendix E for market intelligence Web sites).

Business Is Personal

Doing business in the Arabian Peninsula countries can be very different from conducting business elsewhere in the world. Arabs do not separate business and personal life as is done in the West. Business involves family, personal relationships, and honor. Personal matters take priority so it is essential that business relations are built on personal friendship and trust. This chapter will examine the unique business culture of the countries of the Arabian Peninsula, including business etiquette and contracts.

Organizational Structure

Arab businesses are organized loosely according to social hierarchy patterns. The government oversees general business affairs, especially those conducted by large companies. Well-placed or wealthy people connected to the government chiefs by blood, marriage, or employment are those who coordinate procedures and make decisions. Laborers carry out the tasks associated with various projects and job needs.

As noted above, Arab organizations are high power distance and very hierarchical. There are often several layers in the organization and access to decision makers is difficult. Organizations strive to keep order and are reluctant to empower subordinates. Because of the bureaucracy and excessive rules, often the only way to get things done is through a personal contact.

In Arab organizations there is great dichotomy between managers and subordinates. Those with authority are expected to issue specific instructions and subordinates do not take action without orders.

Arab organizations are much flatter than they are in the West. Typically everyone reports to the owner or manager and has equal access to him. It is common for Arab managers to discuss several issues at the same time with several different people. This may create the appearance of inefficacy, however, in this polychronic culture Arabs are able to operate quite efficiently. This behavior can, however, lead to a lack of confidentiality and a lack of punctuality.

Getting Started

To get started doing business on the peninsula it is a good idea to visit the region to get a feel for the business climate. You can do this by attending a local trade show. However, do not rush into establishing a permanent presence or making an agreement with an agent. Get to know the market and establish your sources of market intelligence. This will likely take several visits.

In preparing to do business in the peninsula countries, you will need to register with the government of the country that you will visit. Sometimes you have to be approved for a business visa before departing your own country, whereas in other cases, you can obtain a visa at the airport. Be sure to find out what is needed before leaving your homeland. In most cases you may be required to hire an agent from the country you plan to visit to represent your interests to that government. Even if it is not required, it is a good idea. If you already have an agent, he can advise you of the red tape that must be cut to enable your firm to establish a legitimate business presence in that nation.

If you do not yet have an agent, contact the government while your project is in the planning stages to find out what is required for your visit and commercial negotiations. You may be able to find the appropriate government office and official on the Web, or you might need to get a referral from someone you know who is already actively doing business in the region. The Economic Section of the American Embassy in the respective country can also provide a list of agents or distributors in the country for your industry (See Appendix E). Be sure to comply with all rules and become familiar with restrictions, limitations, penalties, and fines to avoid unpleasant surprises or sticky circumstances later. An agent can help to guide you through these with minimum difficulties.

Going through the proper channels in the early stages of your business dealings will facilitate the process and clear the way for productive negotiations.

The two main methods of doing business are agency and joint venture.

Agents

There are two types of agents in the region: the sales agent and the commission agent or broker.

The sales agent represents products for a region and gets compensation by a commission on sales or a mark-up on products sold. He is usually an independent businessman who represents several companies and products for the same area. He will often have a showroom and office where he meets with prospective customers and have storage for inventory. Before you choose a sales agent you should consider the following:

- Will the agent buy the product and resell it?
- Will he act as an Original Equipment Manufacturer (OEM)?
- What will the discounted sales price be?
- Will the market support a price to cover your costs and be a value to him?
- What will be his territory?

After answering the above questions, select an agent based on the following areas:

- His reputation for doing business.
- Evidence of reliable business connections with banks, the government, and industry.
- Geographical experience with and knowledge about your target niche.
- History of successful commercial representation and brokering.
- Insight to current market trends and patterns.
- In Saudi Arabia, he must be registered with Ministry of Commerce.
- Arab ancestry and citizenship.
- Preferably cutting-edge knowledge of global business trends and technological development.
- Does he represent competitors?
- Is he someone you would want to do business with? (i.e. Do you trust him?)

The commission agent is a broker who helps you get a contract. He will not be involved in the execution of the deal. They are people with connections who can help you get the deal and are paid a commission for their service. They are an essential part of doing business in the area. Their role is to provide the environment for you to make a contract.

Commission agents will often ask for their commission in advance. However, if you pay in advance you will lose any leverage with him in solving problems that come up later.

Agreements with sales agents normally have to be registered with the government while commission agent agreements usually do not. In fact commission agents will often want the agreement to remain confidential.

Agents often are distributors, importers, or wholesalers. Ask for references or seek a referral from expatriates who are doing business in the Arab state where you are visiting. As with all your business dealings, keep good records about agent relations and actual work performed.[1] This will make it easier to follow up on inquiries or confirm specific practices.

Partnership Benefits

Partnerships in a joint effort manner of speaking (rather than the legal definition) can help to ensure successful outcomes for your enterprise. As in the West, teamwork often accomplishes more than individual effort, if it is managed well.

First, assemble the most suitable employees in your company for commerce in the peninsula states. As discussed previously, you will want to select staff members with traits like the following:

- Strong character
- Patient demeanor
- Cultural sensitivity
- Respectful attitude
- Business savvy
- Global expertise or regional insight

Team members with these attributes will give your firm the best chance of conducting business in the peninsula countries.

Second, enlist a small group of commercial partners who can help your business grow and thrive via their expertise in the following areas:

- Good communication
- Marketing experience
- Customer support skills
- Geographical familiarity with your service area

Qualified importers and distributors frequently have this knowledge and are willing to work with Western firms to mutual advantage. Although some companies delegate all marketing duties to the agent, it is a good idea to stay involved and oversee these important aspects of your business.

Finally, good communications skills are vital for the success of your enterprise. Your agent should be able to clearly discuss with you any questions and concerns, as well as make detailed progress reports. He also needs to be able to communicate effectively with government officials and company representatives via spoken speech and possibly written documents, too.

A Positive Reputation

Successful completion of a business deal will greatly contribute to your reputation and your reputation will determine if you receive other contracts.

Carefully calculate your bids and quotes for business. Americans are known in Arab countries for trying to make big profits. Make sure you charge enough to cover your agent's fee and bid/performance bonds, as well as costs related to materials, labor, subcontracting fees, etc., but don't expect to take advantage of Arab business owners, who are more than willing to consider lower bids from representatives of non-Western countries, especially those in various stages of economic development where such contracts can make a real difference in the economy.

In a business culture that is based on personal relationships as much as professional associations, it is important to project an image of good character rather than a glitzy profile. In the United States and Europe it may seem that "the early bird gets the worm," but in the Arab world, you will do well to remember the fable of the tortoise and the hare with the motto, "slow and steady wins the race."

If you plan to negotiate a large contract or cultivate a long-term business relationship, you will benefit by establishing a local presence in the country where you hope to do business. It is a good idea to open an office that is operated by key staff from the home office. Utilize local workers for unskilled labor needs. Be available for frequent visits (as host or guest) and follow-up to discussions and negotiations.

Women in Business

As discussed earlier in this book, the majority of Arab women spend more time at home than in the workplace. With traditional domestic occupations, their greatest goal is to bear sons through which they will earn status and perhaps wield familial authority. Due to close family ties in the Middle East, children – especially sons – honor their parents, especially the mother as she ages. Indirectly, women can influence their children's decisions and actions in the business world as well as the family circle.

In companies, business, and industry, there are few roles open to women that cannot be managed by men. If a woman does take a public position, she is required by the Qur'an to dress modestly, which means sleeves must cover the elbow, at least; many women (or their male family members) prefer wrist-length sleeves. Long, loose-fitting skirts or trousers are worn, with a head covering that may be a headscarf or body veil. The choice and style of clothing depends on the region as well as the religious practices of the family. Unless you learn otherwise, if introduced to male and female company representatives, regard the man as the person with whom you should conduct business, but do not overlook the woman, extending your hand to shake hers only if she offers it.

During business meetings or social functions, avoid inquiring about or commenting on an Arab woman, such as a man's wife, daughters, or other relatives, unless there is a special reason to do so. Women typically remain in the background of both types of situations, unless you happen to become close friends with a couple, especially if you have brought your wife and the two women get along and enjoy each other's company. In keeping with the attitude of modesty in and toward women, it is best to maintain a discreet personal and professional distance.

Business Relationships

While it is globally understood that networking is essential in developing strong and lasting business associations, the Middle East places particular emphasis on personal relationships as the foundation for business dealings. Stemming from their tribal roots and clan-like connections, Arabs in the business world build a network of people who know each other well and, in many cases, are connected professionally or related personally. Although this may smack of nepotism in the West, to Arabs, professional practice requires the knowledge of and trust in those with whom business is conducted.

If you plan on doing long-term business in the peninsula states, make a point of cultivating friendships with personnel employed by organizations with which you will be establishing relations. You can expect to start slow and build gradually to the level of negotiations that may become productive and mutually rewarding.

Office Protocol

In the typical Arab business office, things tend to run differently than they do in the U.S. or Europe. As mentioned in an earlier chapter, time serves the Arab people; people don't worship time as they do in the West. The workday begins with an early morning start time, a midday break for dinner and a daily nap, and then late afternoon hours from perhaps 4 to 8 p.m. or thereabouts.

Business culture often is more relaxed in the peninsula states. Although people dress formally, visitors usually can recognize hierarchy distinctions between high-ranking and low-ranking employees. Supervisors expect and receive clear-cut respect, while subordinates know and keep their places in the pecking order.

Managers can be very aggressive and direct, or what Westerners might perceive as confrontational. They get into employees' faces, raise their voices, and may even give a forceful push or shove to underscore their words. These behaviors are common to the culture and should not be taken amiss under normal circumstances. It is unlikely that an Arab professional person will take this tack with a Western guest.

The business environment may seem low-key and slow-moving in comparison to fast-paced enterprises in the U.S. and other countries. Employees may appear to be sitting around waiting for something to do, when in reality, they are going about their jobs at a more relaxed pace than many of us are used to. Sometimes they were simply waiting for orders, or they may be expecting the return of a supervisor from abroad or another branch of the company. In a later chapter the role of Islam will be discussed but keep in mind that devout Muslims pray five times daily, typically in a private room away from routine office activities. Unexpected visits from distant guests or family members may also demand a company owner's time and attention during which you may be expected to wait if you are not invited to join.

While it may appear that little to no work is being performed in the office at any given time, it is likelier that events and activities like those described above may be taking place beneath the calm surface, and that work is proceeding at a normal pace.

Work relations frequently are built on personal relationships, so it is important to maintain a casual friendship with those with whom you hope to do business. With a positive attitude and patience, you might become one of those envied guests for whom everyday activities are interrupted and put on hold.

Meetings

Initial meetings are used to build relationships. Plan to engage in conversation and get to know the other person but not make substantial progress.

When organizing a business meeting, it is a good idea to plan ahead for those who should be asked to attend from both the Arab and non-Arab teams. When discussing important decisions, it is wise to have the top negotiators in attendance. This is not the time or place to send a junior official as company representative, unless the meeting will cover non-essential matters. You will want to learn who the decision-maker is

45

for the Arab organization with which you hope to work, and ensure that this person is invited to the meeting and will be able to attend. Although you may have the impression that a more vocal or visual person is running the show, it may be the quiet individual, who speaks little but to whom others defer, who will be the one pulling the strings.

Conducting business meetings in an Arab organization may be frustrating to non-Arab participants. Given the many possible reasons above to interrupt, delay, or cancel a meeting, you may spend considerable time waiting for a meeting to start when in actuality it has been cancelled – and you could be the last to find out. Always call to confirm meetings no more than three days before the meeting and again the day of the meeting if possible.

You may arrive for a meeting on time, only to learn that your Arab hosts are running late, without explanation. If you are kept waiting, do not get frustrated. Arabs are good at reading people and may see this as a sign of weakness that they can take advantage of. It is also possible that making you wait is a negotiation tactic. However, usually it is just the normal course of events in a culture where people have multiple issues competing for attention, not to mention problems with the traffic and heat. With luck, the meeting will begin in due course, with all necessary members present at the same time. Another possibility is the meeting will be put on hold indefinitely – usually until the non-Arab guests decide to arrive late or call in and have a subordinate reschedule for a later time. Flexibility rules in the matter of scheduling and conducting professional meetings. Arrange for taxi service to ensure that you arrive on time and avoid a bad start because, while Arabs are frequently late, they will get a bad impression of Westerners who are late.

When you are ushered into the meeting room, follow your host's lead. There usually will be small talk about non-business topics; this may include family matters or global issues. Don't introduce the purpose for the meeting—let your Arab host do this. Be prepared to listen carefully and take notes. Any documents brought to the meeting could and should be printed in both English and Arabic, but sometimes this does not happen. You will need to jot down key information that may not be available in print form, such as contacts' names, organizational chain of command, business procedures, and networking opportunities.

Expect interruptions at any time. Unlike business meetings in the United States that often begin and end on time with the requisite persons in attendance, and continue without interruption, Arab meetings may be interrupted frequently by the arrival of other business associates, family members, or professional associates. These arrivals may signal a "timeout" for coffee and tea, or the new members, though not part of the planned member group, may be invited to take part in the meeting.

Muslims' five daily prayer times last about 15 minutes each: dawn, noon, mid-afternoon, sunset, and dusk. The Arabs with whom you are meeting may interrupt the meeting to conduct prayer services within the company or attend services at a nearby mosque.

Ramadan is a widely observed holy month in Muslim cultures. During the month, eating, drinking, and smoking may occur only between sunset and sunrise, and thus may interfere with a routine business schedule when people become hungry and tired. The workday can change so that the morning session ends earlier, while the evening session runs later, as people prefer to socialize at this festive yet solemn occasion. It is important to find out when the month is observed so you can plan accordingly. Based on the Islamic calendar of 350 days, the observance of Ramadan is calculated on the moon's phases and changes every year.

During the hot summer months of July and August, many families travel to cooler climates for a vacation, so it may be harder to set meetings and conduct business during this time. If you are in the region during the summer months, it is important to be aware that temperatures can rise to 120 degrees Fahrenheit or higher (50 degrees Centigrade) in the desert climate. There may be sandstorms and excess humidity to deal with. In winter, you can expect cooler temperatures and occasional rain between December and February. Daily work schedules are arranged to avoid extreme weather conditions, especially during the middle of the day in the hottest temperatures, so don't expect to do business at these times.

The typical workday consists of two sessions: morning is from 8 or 9 a.m. until 1:30 to 2:30 p.m., followed by lunch, prayer, and an afternoon nap. The afternoon session goes from 4 or 5 p.m. to 8 or 9 p.m. Meetings will usually take longer than you expect so it is wise to only schedule one meeting or appointment for each session, morning and afternoon. On Friday, the holy day for Muslims, most businesses are closed.

Agendas

Meeting agendas are circular and tend to be flexible. They do not follow a linear pattern as they do in the West. Issues are raised when the time feels right. At a business meeting in New York, for example, a marketing committee may cover several related topics in rapid succession, and defer uncovered topics to the next meeting, but in Arab circles, if there is an official agenda, it may be brief, unorganized, or scarcely noted during the proceedings. Again, the frame of reference is that time serves people, not the other way around. Meetings will cover what the leaders feel is necessary, or whatever they are in the mood to discuss that day, even topics that are not proposed in the agenda. While this type of approach can be frustrating to a task-oriented, time-conscious Westerner, the Arab mindset refuses to be bound by an arbitrary set of purposeful goals. The overarching principle of *inshallah* ("if God wills it") permeates the business environment just as it does in the family. Therefore, the meeting will cover only what God decrees for that day. Follow your host's lead in determining if the meeting has ended when discussions revert to small talk and longer periods of silence ensue.

Be alert to nuances in the culture and in communication. Because Arab people avoid direct confrontations and rejection, your host may seem to approve your proposal, but then you might not hear from him again. Or he could ask for time to consider the idea and fail to follow up with a yes-or-no response. Generally, if you are deferred or put "on hold," chances are that you are being told *no* indirectly. It's a good idea not to be pushy or overly direct if you follow up.

The motivational approach may be more productive than being overly competitive or threatening. Point out the advantages that your company can offer that will benefit your Arab hosts, rather than down-playing advantages given by your competitors. Offer careful attention during the meeting and put forth your best effort to negotiate to mutual advantage. If your hosts respond in like manner, chances are they have become interested and will actively engage in ongoing negotiations to close the deal. If you meet with two individuals, which is typical, keep an eye on the quieter local person rather than someone who asks the questions and does most of the talking. Chances are the quieter person is the decision-maker.

If you are presented with an offer or counter-offer that you cannot accept, be careful about criticizing your host. Diplomacy is greatly valued in Arab culture, and you can help to establish a position of solid character by emphasizing commonalities and advantages rather than differences and problems. While there will be times when you may have to be assertive and direct, always do so courteously, even if your Arab host becomes more vocal, in order to preserve integrity and prevent a complete break-down in negotiations.

Diplomacy

In building a personal and professional relationship with your Arab colleagues during meeting sessions, keep in mind that certain topics are taboo and should be avoided. One is the aforementioned reference to your hosts' female relatives, or Arab women in general. It is considered rude to inquire after women to whom you are unrelated.

Related to this topic is the avoidance of discussing personal family issues or spousal relations. These topics are kept private among Arab families and not casually aired to business acquaintances, especially those from other countries. References to sex, sensuality, or nudity are inappropriate and can have a negative impact on business associations, especially when women are present, but even if they are not. Arabs tend to be conservative in public and do not care to discuss or view lenient attitudes toward loose morals.

Hold off on raising discussions centered on religion or politics, and even cultural distinctions, unless your hosts bring up the topic or you know them well enough to believe they will welcome such discussions. These can be sensitive areas to various people on the peninsula, but not necessarily for everyone.

Another subject to avoid is pushing for a prompt decision. It can take several days or weeks, sometimes even months, for a decision-maker to reveal his response to your proposal. Don't try to hurry things along, as this can cast you in a negative light with your hosts.

It is wise not to criticize the way that Arabs do business, exhibit customs, or arrange their organizational structures. In reality, any type of concerns should be voiced in a low-key manner with a proactive attitude and preferably in a one-to-one meeting conducted out of the hearing of others. This is essential to protecting the dignity of your host, just as he would do the same for any guest.

Whatever your personality style, you will want to maintain a low profile in public and not speak loudly or crudely. Over time, in personal gatherings, such restrictions might ease as people get used to each other, but the public norm is to maintain conservative behavior in clothing, speech, and conduct.

Intermediaries

Foreign firms wishing to conduct business in Arabian Peninsula countries typically hire an agent, as has been discussed earlier. An agent may be an employee of a respected shipping firm or he might be an exporter or importer, that is, someone with knowledge about and connections within the business community of the country in which you are establishing a professional presence. An agent will act as the middleman, or intermediary, between a foreign enterprise and Arab business society by providing services that could include document translation, client representation, marketing expertise, and customer support. You will want to consult with respected foreign and Arab companies to get references of agents who will be a good fit with your organization.

A reputable agent should have professional connections that will help to get whatever job done that you wish to assign, whether it be compiling a customer base, building a product line's reputation and popularity, or developing customer support within a targeted region. He should be a native Arab with strong communication skills and preferably have a college degree, perhaps from a Western university. He should be fluent in English and have some familiarity with Western culture and business protocol. Ideally, he will have several years' experience in the field in which you need his services. He should be able to produce references that support his credentials.

Because cultural differences can lead to misunderstandings no matter how effective an agent may seem, it is a good idea to provide clear written instructions in both English and Arabic through the services of a competent translator. You will want to keep a close eye on the accounting books, not because you don't trust your agent, but to ensure that he understands and abides by your business principles, as gift-giving is common, if illegal, in the peninsula states. It may be helpful to encourage your agent to keep clear records about the tasks he is performing and their outcomes.

Another type of indispensable intermediary you will need while doing business in Arabian Peninsula countries is an effective interpreter, or translator. Plan to interview several to get an idea of their training, experience, and style before you hire someone for your company. Be sure to clarify if the translator's services will be used more in verbal meetings and dialogues or in translating written documents. In addition to bilingual capabilities, a translator should be familiar with the type of business you are in and the cultural distinctions and language barriers that potentially exist between the two countries being represented and translated.

Islamic Banking

Financial matters that are handled through banking institutions are managed differently than you may be accustomed to in the West.

Since usury, or lending money at interest and earning interest with no risk, is forbidden by Islam, commercial Islamic banking was developed in the first half of the last century in Egypt and Pakistan. In the 1970s, it expanded to other Muslim countries. Today many commercial banks in the Middle East, Europe, and North America offer Islamic banking services and their Islamic financial instruments are increasingly accepted around the world.

Islamic banks charge fees rather than interest for their services and rather than paying interest on savings accounts, customers participate in bank investments for a portion of the gain or loss. Current account services are offered with check writing and ATM cards, but charge cards are strictly debit cards. Long-term credit can be arranged by the bank taking ownership and leasing to the customer or the customer making installment payments until he assumes ownership. Banks can also finance a project by becoming a partner and sharing in the profits. This financing model has proven effective in developing countries and has encouraged greater foreign investment.[2]

You will need to consider creative financing options when you propose a costly project. Islamic banks may agree to partner with an investment plan, but they risk their own capital in doing so. Don't expect to apply for a loan to underwrite your company's investment needs. Foreigners need to come prepared with alternative finance options in which Islamic banks may participate as partners.

Business Etiquette

Common courtesy is the rule for business etiquette in Arabian Peninsula countries. More so than in Western regions, humility, conservatism, and preferment of the host are the norms under which business is conducted.

Greetings

If you are used to doing business in the United States or other parts of the West, you may feel uncomfortable when meeting Arab businessmen during your negotiations. Unlike the firm, if brief, handshake that many men exchange in Western countries upon meeting one another, Arab men will add a kiss on one or both cheeks to their handshake if they are particularly well associated or have been absent for some time.

The elderly receive great respect, receiving a younger man's kiss on the forehead or nose instead of his cheek, which reflects the utmost honor. Foreigners do not have to kiss their Arab hosts; a handshake will suffice. Be sure to extend the right hand, not the left, in greeting; using the left hand, used for hygienic purposes, implies an insult.

Information Exchanged in Introductions

Arabs exchange more information when they first meet than Westerners do. They want to determine the social status and connections of the person they are meeting. They may tell about themselves, their family, and their social connections. The information about family and connections is often more important than information about themselves. If you are not as free with this information about yourself, they may think you are hiding something. Also, do not think the information they are giving you is irrelevant, this information may be useful to you later if you need personal contacts.

When you are introduced to several people take the time to complete the greeting customs with each individual. If your greeting is too brief and seems rushed, it will appear you are not interested in the person or in getting his business.

There is also a great difference between Arabs and Westerners as to what is considered personal or private. Arabs will not ask about your female relatives but they will ask you if you are married and if not, why. If you are married and do not have children, they will find that curious and will want to know why. They also like to discuss how much you paid for something or what your salary is. If you are asked a question you do not want to answer, it is best to respond without giving an answer. This is how Arabs would respond to a question they do not want to answer, so after a few minutes they will get the message.

Reciprocal Favors

Reciprocity is important in Arab personal and business relations. On a personal level, if you admire something overmuch, it will appear as though you are asking for it, and the item may well be given to you; your refusal will not be accepted. Therefore, it is a good idea to openly admire something only briefly rather than dwelling on it.

If you present a gift to your Arab friend or host, he may not open it in front of you. Don't be offended; this is customary as a means of saving face or preventing embarrassment. Likewise, if you receive a gift, you do not need to open it until later.

In business relations, the exchange of favors can consolidate a working relationship, although it should be handled carefully. Obviously, taken the wrong way, doing something for someone who has done something for you could suggest bribery or another inappropriate action. In the Arab world, such acts are looked upon differently—rather as a way to cement relations and reward friendship and loyalty rather than taking advantage of an existing "debt." Be careful to spell out expectations and limits when planning a business deal so that misunderstandings do not arise later.

Rules of Business Etiquette
- Be on time. Although Arabs are not punctual, they will expect you to be.
- Dress conservatively. Men are expected to wear business suits.
- Bring business cards. Print business cards with English on one side and Arabic on the other.

- Do not expect a private meeting. It is common for Arabs to meet with several people at once. Also, only senior executives will have private offices, expect to wait in the outer office until the "secretary" tells you to go in.
- As you enter, say *as-salaam Alaykum.*
- Shake hands with the senior man first, then with everyone else in a counter-clockwise direction.
- Take the seat to the right of the official, give up your seat when someone else comes in.
- Accept coffee with right hand when it is served.
- Do not discuss business until your host brings it up.
- Address your counterparts with the appropriate titles.
- Gifts are appreciated but not necessary. Usually gifts are only exchanged among close friends.
- Maintain strong eye contact and expect to sit and stand close together, as both are a sign of trust.
- Be patient. Don't rush to discuss business.
- Do not speak loud in public or appear too animated, it shows a lack of humility.
- Don't assume the person asking the most questions is the decision-maker; often it is the opposite, the least important person. If you ask many questions, they may assume you are not important.
- If you are giving someone a document or money, relay it directly to his hand rather than laying it on the table.
- Arab men may hold hands casually when in public together, which is meant as a gesture of friendly or casual closeness.
- Your Arab associates will sit closer to you than a fellow Westerner might.
- When entering an office or a home where several are present, it is polite to greet each person in attendance; failure to do so is considered impolite and even rude.

Contracts

The Arab culture places more importance on a person's word than on written documents. Therefore, contracts are not seen as binding agreements. However, communicating and negotiating between cultures can lead to misunderstandings, and, in case of legal problems courts will favor the locals. Therefore, the importance of a clear business contract cannot be overstated. Negotiations and transactions can be difficult enough in one's own culture; forming an agreement with someone in another culture can be tricky. That is why you need a clear-cut contract that outlines the terms of agreement to the satisfaction of both parties.

Never rush into a contract agreement. It is first important to understand the cultural backdrop of your target company, along with any nuances that may play a role in establishing conditions and coming to an agreement. If you cannot visit the country or maintain a presence there, send an emissary with the skill and expertise to establish a proactive relationship with the host organization. Keep in mind that negotiations can take time, and be prepared to wait, especially if you hope to maintain ongoing business dealings with the company.

If you feel that you are experiencing bias or unfair practices, politely ask to meet with someone else in the company. It is likely that this type of attitude is isolated and not representative of the organization. Do not engage in a verbal showdown or attempt to assert your individual rights or position.

Be frank and open during negotiations. Make eye contact and maintain a firm presence at the table, albeit with a humble and courteous attitude. Allow silence to surface without feeling that you have to say something to fill the void. Follow your host's lead in making small talk or turning to business topics.

Only sign a contract when you are confident of its meaning and all possible implications. If you are unsure, get clarification from legal counsel rather than jeopardize company interests by signing prematurely. An attorney can be consulted at the beginning of negotiations, during the process, at the point of signing, and at the time of enforcement of the contract's terms. Don't hesitate to seek legal assistance if you feel the contract has been violated or misinterpreted.

What to Include

Contracts may include any or all of the following, along with additional items not shown here:

- Contract date(s)

55

- Identification of parties
- Product and service descriptions
- Unit price
- Key vocabulary terms
- Unit quantity
- Payment methods, mediums, and exchange rates
- Costs and fees (duties, taxes, insurance, handling transport)
- Packing and shipping
- Delivery details
- Transportation methods
- Import/export documentation
- Invoice preparation and delivery
- Inspections
- Indemnities
- Intellectual property rights
- Warranties
- Enforcement and remedies
- Arbitration provisions
- Modification provisions
- Cancellation
- Damages
- Attorney fees
- Force majeure
- Governing law
- Choice of forum
- Notices
- Independent counsel
- Acceptance and execution [3]

Each contract is unique and may require a variable combination of sections like those outlined above. Keep in mind that many peninsula states do not have foreign exchange requirements, which may have a bearing on the mode of payments.

Protect Yourself

Your company may have a template it has used in previous contracts for the same or similar companies. Still, it is important to go over the agreement with a fine-toothed comb to check each detail and point before the document is executed. If a problem should occur and the matter goes to a local court, chances are the magistrate will find against your company and perhaps even you personally rather than the local entity. Civil cases are also frequently settled by reconciliation where both parties accept some guilt.

Depending on the nature of your contractual business, it might be a good idea for your agent, the host company's executive(s), your company's executive(s), and legal counsel at minimum to examine the contract. Additional reviewers may be necessary to clarify the terms of agreement and to identify possible weaknesses or gaps that are open to misinterpretation or exposure.

Must be in Arabic

Contracts must be in Arabic. Of course, you will have an English copy but the Arabic copy is the official contract and will be used in court if that becomes necessary. This is another reason to have your own, good interpreter.

Chapter Four

Negotiating

Conducting business in the Arabian Peninsula can be exciting and productive, but negotiations also can seem unfruitful and frustrating to those who are unfamiliar with the business culture and traditional values. When you conduct business, armed with knowledge about these factors, you can expect to have a meaningful experience. If you have a commission agent, he should also be involved in the negotiation process and advise you on how to handle issues that arise.

Objective vs. Subjective Perspectives

Arab culture tends to view the world as subjective rather than objective. In other words, Arab business leaders interpret news, events, and actions through an individualized lens that allows for differing meanings and applications. A personal perspective carries more weight than factual information. Logical arguments may prove ineffective in the face of contradictory beliefs, especially when personal honor is at stake. It's a good idea never to assume that you and an Arab host or colleagues share the same perceptions. Seek clarification before moving forward, although most Arabs can be direct in offering their opinions.

Arabs are quite good at transacting business. After all, they've been trading for centuries with travelers who visited their seaports or traversed the caravan routes. You can expect Arab negotiations to work toward a goal of selling high and buying low. Of course, all businesspersons take that approach, but Arabs are particularly skilled at it. You will need to strike a delicate balance of maintaining your position on the value of your goods and services while striking a fair bargain that will benefit all parties. Bargaining is an art in the Middle East. You will want to learn how to recognize the nuances of being met with a firm price versus a starting figure.

Family and Connections

The Arab world places premium value on family relationships, and this may carry over into business negotiations. Children are raised affectionately to honor their parents and older relatives. Opinions of the elderly carry great weight. Extended family may be invited to participate in decision-making processes. You will need to observe the family dynamics of your business contact in Arabian Peninsula countries to determine the role of individual or collective groups of family members.

Extended family can play a significant role in business operations. As indicated previously, male relatives may stop in for a visit at any time during business hours, which can interrupt and delay your negotiations. Do not take this as an affront or as diminished interest in your proposal. Arabs view family relations as high priority and usually receive relatives at any time, no matter what type of business is being conducted. The visitor(s) may stay for coffee, tea, and news before going on their way, when your negotiations will continue.

Connections play a vital role in Arab society, both in personal and business matters. As discussed in Chapter Three, you will need an agent, or sponsor, to facilitate business transactions in the peninsula. Other connections may serve the purpose, as well. For example, it helps to make the acquaintance of other dealers, companies, and representatives in the region who eventually may be playing a role in your enterprise. Your agent can introduce you to the key persons you should meet. Your Arab host or business contact also may be instrumental in detailing the chief persons with which to become acquainted. Don't pass up an opportunity to meet relevant contacts when you are invited to business functions or personal entertainment events. While Westerners are aware of the value of cultivating a wide range of business associates, in Arab culture this is even more important due to the traditional communal aspects of Middle Eastern society.

Persuasion

Persuasion, of course, is an intrinsic aspect of marketing. Doing business in the Arab world, you will need to become familiar with regional methods of persuasion that are acceptable and considered neither too forward nor too passive.

The love of communicative eloquence is an intriguing characteristic in Arab business negotiations. Lofty metaphors, localized idioms, and figurative parallels can sound very foreign to a Western businessperson that is accustomed to straightforward language and technical jargon. You probably will encounter an interesting mix of language styles when you negotiate business deals in Arab society. In particular, persuasion will emphasize friendship, personal appeals, and emotional arguments.

1. **Friendship.**

   In the West, it is often said that business and pleasure (personal relationships) do not mix. In the Arab world, the opposite is true. Arab business frequently is conducted in part or in whole during pleasurable experiences like visiting at home or dining out. Even regularly scheduled business meetings at the office can take on the feeling of a comfortable social atmosphere when friends and relatives stop by for a casual visit that temporarily interrupts proceedings. Friendship ties can lead to the expectation of reciprocal favors: "If I do this for you, will you do something for me?" This mindset is a throwback to the era when tribes and clans formed liaisons and alliances through the exchange of mutual favors in order to survive chaotic social conditions and a harsh environment. Do not be affronted if your Arab contact seems to be asking for favors or offering you special assistance, with the implication a return favor might be expected, unless it is insinuated in a dark or threatening way that includes illegal activity.

2. **Personal appeals.**

   Famed for their hospitable welcome and ready acceptance of guests, whether for personal or business visits, Arabs build strong social bonds with their visitors as a means of instilling trust and promoting mutually beneficial ties. Although Westerners generally differentiate between personal and business connections to avoid criticism for favoritism, nepotism, or pandering, Arab businessmen prefer to get acquainted with someone fairly well before doing business with that person. This means that you may develop a friendship that runs parallel to your business relationship. As a result, you may be approached with a personal appeal, not just a professional request. As long as it is made in an above-board way that does not breach professional protocol, you should feel honored by your host's trust in you that leads to such requests. Never promise more than you can deliver, of course, or presume upon a relationship that might be still very tenuous.

3. **Emotional arguments.**
Due to longstanding Arab linguistic eloquence, you can expect to be confronted by emotional arguments at the height of negotiations. Voices may be raised, fists could be slammed, and subordinates might even get shoved. Not to worry. This just means that the issues are being sincerely debated and that things are moving along in a productive way toward the end goal. Your role is to remain calm and steady, without flinching, while continuing to speak in a respectful tone and stand by the merits of your proposition. This doesn't mean you cannot haggle – in a professional manner, naturally – but don't move so far from your original position that your Arab associates may deem you untrustworthy. Measure your end goal against your starting point for a reasonable amount of give-and-take, but don't go all over the map in restating or redefining your position. Give and expect respect to reach a dignified conclusion.

Time Requirements

Business deals in many parts of the world can occur at a speedy rate. A salesperson makes a call and sometimes closes the deal in a 30-minute visit. The parties hardly know each other and may never meet again except for follow-up business, if that should occur.

But in the peninsula states, business is transacted at a much slower pace. Established on mutual trust and respect, business negotiations take time in a culture where time is of little consequence. The West lives by the clock; this is not so in the Middle East.

Be prepared for the long haul. You will need a reliable agent, good connections, and much patience to transact business on the peninsula. Expect to put in a fair amount of time getting to know your hosts as they become acquainted with you, and in discussing proposals that could lead to a rewarding deal.

Doing business in the region can be time-consuming. Expect slow or no movement while you establish friendships and build trust. Sometimes this happens more quickly with younger, Western-educated government and business leaders. In any case, do not try to rush a contractual agreement or purchasing decision, which can require several meetings over a period of one to two weeks, or even longer. Working through your agent may take several months before operations are approved and established.

Although you won't necessarily have to attend numerous meetings, you can rely on the fact that those in which you participate may be long and drawn out. Interruptions could be plentiful, but don't be put off when guests stop in for coffee and a chat. Hospitality and generosity are strong virtues in Arab culture. The better you acclimate and the degree to which you accommodate these virtues can make a difference in the success or failure of your venture.

Negotiations and Social Activities

While exercising patience over a series of meetings during which your proposition is under consideration, you may be invited to participate in any number of social activities related to your host's personal life or business interests. Frequently, the two will overlap. Although the combination of professional and personal interests is not exclusive to the Arab business world, it differs from the way social activities are navigated in Western societies.

In the West, company representatives talk business at speaker breakfasts, golf outings, and dinner meetings. But in Arab society, business is put on the back burner during a social activity. You should avoid embarking on a business discussion while visiting your host at home, at least until after everyone has enjoyed a meal or coffee. Even then, you will need to wait for the right time, which sometimes can be signaled by the host. If you know him well, however, and feel that he is ready to discuss your proposition, you can introduce it in a low-key way.

Family parties, dinner celebrations, and special events are reserved for fun and relaxation. You should not try to discuss business unless invited to do so by your host. However, in addition to the enjoyment and pleasure such activities bring when you are not conducting business, they also provide excellent opportunities for getting to know your Arab associates in a more personal way, which lays a firm foundation for conducting business at the office in the style that Arabs prefer.

Interruptions

Westerners that have been influenced by a "me-first" culture may find it difficult to take a back seat to other guests, family members, and friends while doing business on the peninsula. Stemming from the time-honored traditions of hospitality and respect, Arabs welcome those who come to visit at home or at the office at almost any time (siestas notwithstanding). Just when you feel that you have your host's attention and he is seriously considering your proposal, your meeting can be interrupted by an affectionate child, an inquiring wife, a subordinate seeking instructions, a family member who has come to pay respects, or a guest from another company or representing another purpose. This does not mean that your host values you less; it only reflects the common attitude of welcoming those who submit themselves to the host's guidance or seek his hospitality. Your visit may be temporarily suspended, but it will resume when the guests have been received, entertained or fed, and have departed.

Consequently, to maximize your chance of getting the best reception and hearing for your business proposal, try to arrange your visit when others are less likely to interrupt, although sometimes this is hard to gauge. An early morning appointment may be helpful, as well as one following the siesta, especially if your purpose is focused and pressing. Otherwise, schedule a time when others might pop in and use those interruptions as an example of your adaptability and good nature, which your host is likely to notice.

Information Exchange and the First Offer

Like an artful dance or carefully arranged musical composition, international negotiation should follow a series of steps that bridge cultural gaps and lead to productive outcomes. The following successful model is outlined by John B. Cullen and K. Praveen Parboteeah in *Multinational Management: a Strategic Approach:* [1]

1. Preparation.
2. Building the Relationship.
3. Exchanging Information and the First Offer.
4. Persuasion.
5. Concessions.
6. Agreement.
7. Post Agreement.

Step #3, Exchanging Information and the First Offer, is the exchange of what both parties want from the transaction. This usually is made as a formal presentation, or proposal, and is considered to be the "first offer." Each country's culture varies in the type, amount, and level of information that is exchanged initially and what percent of the goal the first offer will be.

In U.S. negotiations, information exchange is given directly and briefly. However, in Arab societies, the offer grows out of the business relationship, which needs to be established as a preliminary step. Few technical details are discussed at this point. The first offer or counteroffer moves transactions to between 20% and 50% of the goal. This amount of movement is greater than many cultures, including the U.S. where the first offer is typically 5-10% off the "real" goal, reflecting the extreme Arab starting point. [2]

At this stage of negotiations, participating parties will be presented with a general overview of each side's position and goals. The resulting framework enables ongoing negotiations to continue through persuasion and additional steps toward final decisions.

Negotiating Strategies Used by Arabs and Counter Strategies

As in Western negotiations, persuasive strategies come in a variety of forms, some positive and others punitive. As a general rule, avoid coercion tactics like these:

- Threat: If things don't go my way, I will play tough.
- Warning: If you do something with which I disagree, I will respond negatively.
- Punishment: I will do something you don't like, such as end negotiations abruptly.
- Command: You have no choice but to do as I say.
- Interruption: I will talk when you do or keep you from talking.

Strategies like these can lead to losing face, which is strictly inappropriate in Arab culture. On the other hand, the following approaches may be usable in suitable contexts:

- Promise: I will help you if you help me.
- Recommendation: I will help good things happen for you if we come to an agreement.
- Reward: I will do something that you will appreciate (without conditions).
- Commitment: I will follow through on our agreement.
- Self-disclosure: I will be open about myself or the company to help you understand the importance of this deal.[3]

As you become more familiar with Arab culture, you will develop better understanding about the ways in which business is conducted in order to achieve mutually beneficial goals. Above all, never resort to underhanded measures or shortcuts to achieve your goals, as they can lead to aborted negotiations or even legal charges when they become known.

When negotiating with Arabs you will encounter five primary negotiating strategies or styles. In trade, Arabs tend to come across as impassive, arrogant, and social. Regarding investments, they project a hierarchical or stern manner.[4] Here are the five common negotiating strategies or styles used by Arabs, along with suggestions for countering them:

1. **Impassive**: The impassive negotiator creates the image of being indifferent, he does not seem to care if he wins or loses. If they are the buyer, this causes the seller to go to extremes to get a reaction. If they are the seller, their impassivity gives the impression that they have many buyers and can set their own

price and choose from among the buyers, causing the buyer to raise his price to beat the competition.

Counter the impassive strategy by being pragmatic. Do extensive research and have a complete, detailed plan with options for you and your counterpart. Lay out the plan early in the negotiations and let your opponents choose an option. Be careful, however, not to dismiss their ideas and cause them to lose face.

Another counter-strategy for the impassive strategy is brinkmanship. Brinkmanship involves threatening to break off discussions unless an issue is resolved.

A third counter-strategy is to overwhelm them. If you are the buyer, offer a price they can't refuse. If you are the seller, overwhelm them with information, addressing all their concerns.

The final impassive counter-strategy is to wear them down with technical data. You want them to realize the limits of their knowledge without making them lose face. Ensure your interpreter is well versed on the data.

2. **Arrogant**: Arrogance is unconscious behavior on the part of the negotiator. It is caused by feeling inferior or not realizing that you are making your counterpart feel inferior. It can be countered by concealing your inadequate feelings about yourself, your product, or company and by understanding your counterpart's viewpoint and convincing them that you are equals.

Because Arab wealth stemming from 20th century oil discoveries followed a period of European overview and control, the people may seem to project a distant, detached, or arrogant persona in an effort to set themselves apart as special or unique. A general understanding of regional history in the post-World War II era can greatly help Westerners understand and deal with this attitude.

An arrogant strategy can be countered by exploiting weakness. This requires careful research before negotiations begin and studying counterparts during the meeting to identify any weakness.

A second counter-strategy is called "compliant." The compliant strategist makes concessions early in the process. The arrogant negotiator is then drawn into the process, thinking concessions will continue. However, the compliant negotiator saves some major points for the end then demands compensation for earlier concessions. The arrogant negotiator is forced to grant the concessions or face the possibility of losing everything. This counter-strategy will only work when you are host, so your counterpart also has time pressure to return home.

Social strategy is described below; however, it can also be used as a counter-strategy against a counterpart who has an arrogant style. Social activities are used to build relationships and friendships so you can operate on an equal basis.

Stern is also an Arab strategy and is described below. It can be used as a counter-strategy against arrogant negotiators by hiding a lack of confidence and making the two sides feel equal.

3. **Social**: Arab negotiators will take full advantage of the social and hospitality aspects of their culture during negotiations to win over their counterparts. Business can be conducted only after a social framework has been erected. Plan on spending time getting to know your Arab hosts before getting down to business. This can take time, but is worth it in the long run. There may be dinners at exclusive restaurants, tickets for sporting events, receptions with high-ranking officials, and invitations to family parties. This socialization is used to become friends and cement relationships before a contract is signed. However, the combination of jet lag and late-night socialization can wear you down, cause you to make mistakes, or reveal too much information. The social strategy can be hard to resist, especially when you are far from home. Know the local social decorum so you do not offend and do not let your guard down. Friendship will be sincere, but it can also be a strategy.

    Social strategy can be countered with intimidation. You must instill fear without them being aware of the process or losing face. Often it can be achieved with subtle comments suggesting you understand how important the deal is to them or how terrible it would be if they lost a market.

    Exploitation is another counter strategy to the social strategy. It involves exploiting weaknesses. Be careful not to use too much; no one likes to be exploited, and they will not tolerate it if they get the impression you are trying to exploit them.

The stern strategy is described below. You can counter the effects of the social strategy by only doing the minimal required social activities and not appearing to be affected by them, rather, you just stick to business.

Impassive strategy is described above and is also a good counter-strategy for the social strategy.

Deception is a strategy used in some degree by all negotiators. It is never wise to let your opponent know your entire plan. However, it should only be used in small amounts and only in the short term if you want to build a lasting relationship. For example, you may lead them to believe the trust, friendship, or relationship is something other than what it is until the desired time.

4. **Hierarchical**: The hierarchical style is a team approach. It involves sending all decisions through the chain of command. As previously noted, Arab organizations are very hierarchical and negotiators will not have authority to make compromises. Identify the decision-maker early on. If he is not present, save some concessions for when you meet with him.

Hierarchies can be countered with a consensus. Consensus negotiators are united. They make a plan in advance and do not deviate from it. When faced with a consensus, hierarchies collapse in the face of overwhelming unity and organization.

Hierarchies can also be countered with a horizontal strategy. This involves attacking on several fronts simultaneously, thus overloading the decision-maker.

A third counter-strategy is to exploit dissentions or disloyalty, causing the hierarchal structure to crumble.

5. **Stern**: The stern negotiator uses discipline to control the meeting. This style will be obvious from the beginning. They will be serious and want to get right down to business. They are usually older and seem grumpy and use this style to intimidate. However, it only works on people who let it. Remember it is just a style and focus on the substance.

Arab negotiators may display a façade of shrewdness. A stern expression or impassive attitude may cover uncertainty or confusion in Arabs during business negotiations. It is best not to challenge this image, but rather make use of the opportunity to clarify information and add needed details that may help to clear up misunderstandings and pave the way to agreement.

Exploitation, pragmatic and technical strategies as described above can also be used to counter the stern strategy.

The following table summarizes the negotiation strategies used by Arabs and counter strategies you can use against them. [5]

Arab Negotiation Strategies	Counter Strategies
Impassive	Pragmatic Brinkmanship Overwhelming Technical
Arrogant	Exploitive Compliant Social Stern
Social	Intimidating Exploitive Stern Impassive Deceptive
Hierarchical	Consensus Horizontal Exploit dissent
Stern	Exploitive Pragmatic Technical

Arabs tend to have extreme marketing ranges. Very high asking prices and very low selling prices may seem insulting to Westerners, but this is a common Arab strategy for establishing a flexible range for negotiation, so don't be put off by it.

During breaks in negotiations, your team should meet and determine which strategy is being used by your counterparts and, if necessary, change your counter strategy. An advantage Westerners have over Arabs is that Westerners can quickly change strategies, especially Americans.

Awareness of history, customs, attitudes, and taboos can greatly enhance your chance of success. Also, avoid bringing women to negotiations. Females play a marginal role in Arab business affairs. In fact, only women of status or financial standing hold any real authority, and they are rare. Plan to leave women out of your negotiations in deference to Arab preferences. If you insist on bringing females along, be sure they comply with local dress and behavior codes.

Negotiating Tactics Used by Arabs

Once you have decided on a negotiating strategy you must choose your tactics. You should choose tactics that support your strategy. All of the above-mentioned strategies can also be used as tactics. The difference is that tactics are temporary and can frequently change while strategy is long-term. In addition to the above strategies, the following are some other tactics Arabs will use in negotiations.

1. Walking out or terminating the meeting is an obvious sign that the negotiating is going badly. Because of the reluctance to say "no," it may be an indirect way of rejecting your offer. However, it could also be merely a tactic to get you to make more concessions.

2. As discussed earlier, meetings with Arabs can involve long periods of silence. Because many Arabs are aware of the stress that these long periods can cause Westerners, they may deliberately create silent periods when negotiating in order to cause embarrassment and get a concession from the other side. You should be prepared to fall silent.

3. Another tactic is to keep you waiting for a meeting. Some waiting will be normal, but it could also be a tactic your counterpart is using against you to weaken or test you. Don't wait too long or you will appear desperate.

4. Bluffing involves deliberate lies or deception as to their true intentions. The best way to deal with bluffing is to point out what you think is happening. Also, do not give concessions based on future promises but on what they are putting on the table now.
5. Arabs will use personal pleas to make a deal. The socializing phase is used to build a personal relationship, then they plea with you as a friend and feign hurt feelings if they do not get the deal. Respond to this by keeping in mind the true nature of your relationship (Are you really "old friends?").

Arabs may use pressure tactics against you; however, pressure tactics will not work against Arabs and will only cause suspension. Western pressure tactics differ markedly from those in Arab countries. It is important to understand the differences and negotiate accordingly. Use of the following is common throughout the U.S. and parts of Europe:

- Rush to make a deal or follow up for confirmation. (I can run a credit check right now.)
- Time constraints. (This is a limited offer.)
- Competitive threats. (We have two other companies who want to bid on this project.)

But in the Arab business world, these pressure tactics are useless. In fact, rather than facilitate a deal, they will serve only to alienate your Arab host and squelch any possible agreement you otherwise might have reached.

Since time serves the Arabs, rather than the other way around, there is no rush on their part to reach agreement or confirm an offer. As discussed previously, the negotiating process can take weeks. Competition and limitations may not work in your favor if your Arab hosts feel that you are trying to manipulate them. If they know you have time constraints, they will use it against you by stalling to put pressure on you. If you have a return flight scheduled, do not reveal the scheduled departure date.

Rather than attempt to pressure the company to make a decision, remain pleasantly patient. Your hosts will appreciate the fact that you deem them worthy of your time and are considerate of their need to closely evaluate the situation. You are more likely to reach a positive outcome if you don't try to rush the deal. In addition, using pressure tactics or giving the impression that you want a fast agreement will cause suspicion and be viewed as a sign of a bad deal.

The only tactic that is not permissible is causing your counterpart to lose face, except, of course illegal tactics.

What Are the Limits?

Illegal tactics will vary by country so you should be familiar with the laws of the country you are operating in. However, there are certain tactics that are almost universally forbidden and should never be used. American negotiators are also restricted by the Foreign Corrupt Practices Act.

Some unsavory tactics that you should not use but may encounter are surveillance, extortion, detainment, fraud, stealing, physical force, and bribery.[6]

Host or Guest?

When transacting business in a foreign country, the visitor faces hardships that can weight in the host's favor. Time spent arranging the trip, traveling to the host destination, getting settled and oriented, recovering from fatigue or jet lag, and preparing for a meeting in a foreign environment are some of the initial challenges faced by the traveler. Then there is the matter of arranging for various types of support or checking prearranged services to be sure they function as needed. These include local travel arrangements, an interpreter, agent services, lodging and accommodations, money transfer or credit access, and clerical support, such as copying, fax, and computer equipment as needed.

No matter how much preparation has been made for the trip, no one knows exactly what to expect upon arrival. The language you studied on CDs may sound vastly different when spoken "live" on the street. Your agent may have differing ideas of when and how the first meeting should proceed. And the hours of operation or availability of equipment may prove substandard or non-existent, in some cases. After managing these issues, the visitor still needs to find time and energy to appear his best at the forthcoming meetings.

The host enjoys the home advantage on many fronts: ease with language, culture, accommodations, amenities, meeting space, agenda and pace, etc. It is incumbent on the guest to adapt as quickly and smoothly as possible to ensure that negotiations proceed in a timely and effective manner.

The host/guest dynamics applies not only to the country in which to hold the negotiations, but also to locations of meetings after you arrive. Because of Arab hospitability customs, sometimes it may be to your advantage to be a guest and at other times you may want to be the one visited. If you have a problem with someone it is better to discuss it as a guest because of Arab hospitality rules for guests. You should consider the tactical advantages of being the host or guest based on the occasion.

Haggling: The *Suq* Model

The desire to make a good bargain to one's advantage is a universal goal enjoyed throughout all global cultures. In the Middle East and particularly Arab societies, however, the art of negotiation, or haggling, to get the best possible deal is a goal in and of itself. The *suq* (market) model of haggling structures a social activity within a commercial framework.

Since the days of antiquity, trading and selling have been exciting and important activities on which economic survival depended. But in regions where encampments, towns, and even cities might lie at considerable distance from each other, the arrival of caravans, traders, and merchants raised everyone's spirits with opportunities to get news from abroad, view new wares, and catch up on social activities with old acquaintances who had not been seen in a while. Business often took second place to the relational aspects of market days. That festive air persists even in Western culture today when people visit flea markets or farm markets to check out the products and to visit with neighbors or sellers.

Thus, while haggling, or debating, over the quality and price of merchandise is a commercial activity in its own right that spans countless centuries and most continents, the art of haggling as a way of re-newing acquaintances or forming new business associations exists as a separate but related activity that enjoys a special place in Arab culture. For an American corollary, think of the old-time general store where the senior citizens gathered to catch up on local gossip or exchange news, or the trading post that drew distant trappers and hunters not only to sell their catch but to "chew the fat" by exchanging fish stories and tall tales. Such is the social environment that nurtures the *suq* model of haggling in Arab culture today.

To be successful at haggling, one must understand the market in which the product is poised, along with its value among others of its kind. A price range should be determined and accepted by both parties so that neither offends the other by asking too high or bidding too low. In *suq* dealings, a seller might offer tea, coffee, or other refreshments to the buyer. He might even invite him home for a visit or meal. Inter-spersed with give-and-take over the product will be casual banter and friendly chat about other things. This is how buyer and seller get to know one another and form lasting business connections. The same ba-sic pattern applies for business negotiation.

Whether you are in the Arab marketplace or office, don't expect to make a hasty purchase or sale. The process could be drawn out and lengthy, so settle in for the long haul and enjoy!

Bribes

Making illicit payments – bribery – to facilitate business dealings in an Arab state is designated as illegal, but nonetheless occurs fairly regularly. In employing an agent to represent your business affairs in peninsula countries, you are responsible for monitoring his actions and ensuring that no such payments exchange hands when service agents utilize middlemen for information or to smooth a deal. Well-organized financial records and contractual agreements will help to control this potential problem. Bribery technically occurs when you pay, or allow an agent to pay, someone to facilitate business transactions or to award you a business contract.

If discovered, bribes can result in serious criminal charges. At the very least, you will be charged with improper conduct and lose face in the Arab business community, compromising your professional reputation.

While it's true that a certain amount of bribery is known to change hands at various levels of business, it is legally strictly forbidden. For example, in Saudi Arabia, Royal Decree Number 38 forbids bribery of public servants. Evidence of its existence is difficult to substantiate. You should never engage in bribery or sanction its use in your agent or other representatives. American businessmen are held accountable by the U.S. Foreign Corrupt Practices Act. Make sure you maintain clear, accurate records of all transactions. Do not pay middlemen or offices of any kind to procure business for your company.

While the term *baksheesh* is more common in Egypt, you may occasionally hear it used. However, you should not confuse it with a bribe. It is closer to tipping but is more than just a reward for good service. Since wages are low for laborers, they depend on *baksheesh* to supplement their income and may not perform a service without first receiving it (See Tipping in Chapter Six).

Wherever you plan to do business on the Arabian Peninsula, find out what the law says about bribes and follow the law to the letter.

Saving Face

In Western society, it is common for males to verbally and even physically spar with each other as a way of building camaraderie. In Arab culture, sparring may create friction. Take care not to say or do anything that could cause your host embarrassment or the possibility of losing face during negotiations.

Arabs place great value on traits like honor and respect. To jest coarsely or to use vulgar language, stereotypes, one-upmanship, or a competitive attitude may ensure that you remain an outsider rather than a key player in Arab commerce. Avoid criticizing, directly or indirectly, anything your Arab host says or does. Do not place him or his offers, coworkers, gifts, etc., in a negative position.

Shame or embarrassment will cause bad feelings and possibly lead to an abrupt break in negotiations or the loss of a deal. Do everything in your power to show respect to your Arab counterparts at all times and to maintain honor in the negotiation process.

Avoiding heavy-handed sales tactics is wise, as these go against traditional business culture. If you press for a quick decision, you not only might lose the deal, but also lose favor with the company overall and forestall opportunities for future negotiations.

Rejections

It is not difficult to miss a rejection in Arab business. Usually the rejection is indirect. The speaker may be loud, repetitive, and critical to the point of seeming rude, only to do an about-face and clinch the deal with the right adjustments. On the other hand, low-key agreement and lack of follow-up may really mean *no*, which the other party will learn only gradually, over time.

Conversely, Westerners tend to say *no* directly, usually once. Since that approach comes across as tentative in Arab business, you may be re-approached with the same offer, or the deal may be deemed still open if you do not emphasize your position as rejection.

Non-verbal communication provides a context for interpreting verbal exchanges. Note the following to help you understand what is actually being said:

- Is the person's expression serious, scoffing, or vague?
- Are the eyes focused on you or on a different point of vision?
- To what degree are hand gestures involved?
- Is the voice elevated or soft?
- Is the tone emotional or calm?
- Is there an air of finality or expectation?

Since the Arab language tends to be vague and speakers try to fit words to ideas in ways that can be difficult to translate literally, it is important to consider the non-verbal part of the communicated message so that you can make an appropriate response.

Typically, the chief decision-maker will not engage directly and personally in the haggling process, but rather, leave that to a subordinate. When the decision-maker finally responds to the deal, you will be able to determine whether he is accepting, negotiating, or rejecting an agreement.

The rejection might come as a soft affirmation. In other words, your host might appear to agree to the proposition but then fail to confirm or act on it. He might simply fade into the background of his organization or shift discussion to other matters. This can be confusing and frustrating to the Western businessperson until you understand Arab culture where this type of rejection is the norm that helps to save face and avoid conflict.

The decision may not be directly stated. If you find that your host delays a commitment or gives you a tenuous positive decision, chances are he is practicing evasion that really means *no* to your deal. Don't force the matter, as Arabs dislike confrontation or pushiness, although they sometimes can be pushy to others. There may be another opportunity in the future for you to reshape your offer or to try again.

Communication Uncertainties

In addition to adapting to the Arabic language by speaking through an interpreter, trying to understand your host's English, or making yourself understood in Arabic, related issues can complicate the communication process. The following are common ways in which negotiations can get sidetracked.

1. **Exaggeration.** Although many Western businesspersons make a point of being simplistic or straightforward during negotiations, this is not the case in the Arabian Peninsula region. Elaborate language symbolism includes the use of exaggeration to inflate ideas and emphasize positions. Westerners need to be able to sift through exaggeration to find the literal meaning behind the words.

2. **Silence.** Americans in particular are not comfortable with prolonged silence, especially in professional communication. They often rush to fill conversation gaps, which can work to their listeners' advantage when they unwittingly reveal motives, details, and explanations for surface-level information. Arabs, on the other hand, invoke silence to reflect on the proposition at stake or to mark a transition to another topic of conversation.

3. **Reluctance to say "no."** In tandem with cultural virtues of honor, respect, and hospitality, Arabs avoid saying *no* directly

as well as sidestep difficult decisions and negative information. A tentative *yes* actually may represent a *no* decision. This can mislead a Westerner who accepts a *yes* response at face value and becomes confused when the deal falls through or is delayed.

With time, effort, and concentration, non-Arab negotiators can learn to navigate conversational markers like these to accurately interpret their host's view or position.

Characteristics of the Successful Negotiator

To cultivate a respected position as an effective negotiator in the Arab world, Westerners should learn to embrace and practice the following attributes:

- Uphold the virtues of honor and respect. Treat your Arab host in this manner, and earn a credible reputation that will result in your receiving similar treatment.
- Become informed of appropriate public, professional, and personal behavior and customs, and follow them by observing your host and the people around you.
- Study communication strategies. Learn the verbal and non-verbal cues that will help you understand what is being said and how to respond. Timing, location, and approach can make a distinct difference in the outcome of your transactions.
- Engage in the art of *suq* haggling, when appropriate, incorporating social activities with your business objectives.
- Maintain honest dealings with your host, agent, representatives, and customers. Follow the law and do not try to circumvent traditional practices or current customs.
- Build a personal relationship as a foundation for your professional negotiations. Get acquainted with your Arab host before attempting to conduct business.
- Stay calm when you become frustrated, confused, or disappointed in the way that matters are proceeding. Chances are things are better than they look, but even if not, preserve a professional, trustworthy image for future negotiations.

Finally, when choosing your negotiation team, it is wise to choose members with certain personal characteristics that will enhance your chances of success. The successful negotiator will be someone who is comfortable in a multicultural environment and is good with interpersonal relationships. He should also be tolerant of ambiguity, flexible, have a good sense of humor, have good stamina, have empathy, be curious, and be bilingual if possible. However, being bilingual does not mean someone understands the culture. It is more important to understand how the culture affects negotiation style than the language.[7]

Chapter Five

Business Tips

Doing business on the Arabian Peninsula is rewarding in many ways. Opportunities to explore a new culture, meet warm and welcoming people, and develop an intercultural perspective on negotiations are worth the effort it takes to meet challenges that come with the territory.

This chapter relates practical information that will be useful in understanding how Arabs conduct business. Professional and technical communication, document preparation, and people skills are some of the topics that will be covered.

Professional Communication

Unlike the U.S. and other parts of the West where being direct and saving time is of utmost importance, Arab business culture proceeds slowly and gradually, building on a social network of trust and respect. The spoken word is more important than the written word, so a contract generally serves as a fallback arrangement if the terms fall through. Otherwise, a verbal agreement sealed with a handshake is how most deals are made, with the contract consulted only in the event of conflict. Preceding a meeting with a written document reflects a formal attitude that may present obstacles to the social protocol of building a business relationship. Following a meeting with notes, minutes, or memos is more acceptable.

With respect to the technical aspects of verbal communication, come prepared with knowledge of telephone etiquette as well as culture-appropriate Internet, email, and fax use. All peninsula countries are rapidly developing technological expertise. There are a few things to keep in mind when relying on technical devices and equipment.

Telephone Etiquette

If you are calling someone after business hours, you should only call on the cell phone, not the home phone. If you do not know the person well, you can call until 9 p.m. Friends you may call until 11 p.m. Also, you should not call during the five prayer times or during nap time in the afternoon. (In Yemen, they do not take afternoon naps, but they chew *kot* in the afternoon, so calls will not be productive.)

Here is how a typical phone call might sound. Note the emphasis on personal greetings:

You are calling Ahmed to confirm a meeting. If you know he speaks English, you may switch to English anytime, but the conversation will be the same and the initial greeting should still be in Arabic. The Westerner may find it strange that the caller does not identify himself at the outset; courtesy, manners, and formality take priority.

Ahmed:	Hallo (or *Salam alakum*)
You:	Hallo (or *Wa alakum salam*) *(Reply with same greeting he answers with.)*
You:	*Aasalam alakum* (Peace be upon you)
Ahmed:	*Wa alkum salam* (And upon you be peace)
Ahmed:	*Man maai* (Who is with me?)
You:	*Anna* Steve (I am Steve)
Ahmed:	*Marhaba* Steve. *Anna* Ahmed (Hello, Steve. I am Ahmed)
You:	*Marhaba* (Hello)

If someone other than Ahmed answers the phone, you can ask for Ahmed: "Wyane Ahmed?" When Ahmed comes to the phone, you start all over again.

You:	*Kayf haloka*? (How are you?) (Be effusive with those you know.)
Ahmed:	*Zein, wa anta*? (Fine, and you?)
You:	*Zein* (Fine.)
Ahmed:	*Kayf eltak* (How is your family?)
You:	*Zein* (Fine.)
Ahmed:	*Kayf sehetak* (How is your health?)
You:	*Zein* (Fine.)
You:	*Agool, mita egtima ilyum*? (Tell me, what time is the meeting today?)
Ahmed:	*Bad-ain zuhr*. (After the noon prayer.)

You: *Shukran, asufak badain.* (Thank you. See you later.)
Ahmed: *Afwan* (You're welcome)
You: *Ma salama* (Good-bye.)
Ahmed: *Ma salama*

After a few conversations, you soon will fall into this pattern of telephone greeting and communication that is casual and easy to adopt. Be assured that many Arabs know at least some English, so you should have no problem making your desired telephone connection.

The more telephone calls you receive and make, the easier your conversations will become. You can consult an Arab language guidebook to pick up a few basic phrases for telephone and in-person pleasantries. Appendix D also contains a list of common business terms with Arabic translations. If you can use a few of these words in conversation, your Arab associates and friends are sure to appreciate the effort you put toward assimilating into their culture.

Telephone, Fax, and News Media

Long distance telephone calls can be made in most towns or cities throughout the Arabian Peninsula at the central telephone office. Telecommunications networks include International Direct Dialing (IDD), thanks to satellite links. The usual cost for international calls is US$2 to US$3 per minute, with sporadic weekend reductions. You can use coins and phone cards at most public phone booths, and credit cards in others. Larger hotels provide international telephone service but at a very high price, and of course, you can use your cell phone (called a "mobile" in the Middle East) if you have long-distance service, though you may have to pay a hefty per-minute rate. You may also be able to buy a SIM card for your phone, but if you are visiting several countries you might have to buy one for each country. If you are only making a few calls, the cost per call would be very expensive. Another option is buy an inexpensive pay-as-you-go international phone. This way you can keep the same number and do not have to use hotel phones or buy SIM cards. I have used the Mobal phone with good success in the Middle East (See Appendix E for Web site). You can also rent a phone, usually at the airport.

Pay phones often provide long distance features, or you can use a phone card (for example, Salma) that can be bought at supermarkets and bookstores. International calling booths are located on several street corners throughout the region. STC operates a GSM mobile phone service.

Internet telephones are also an excellent option. You can call anywhere in the world for a few cents a minute. And you can receive calls to the same U.S. number as you travel. (See Appendix E for phone companies).

Fax machines are widely available at telephone offices as well as in major hotels and many companies. Internet services are outdistancing the use of faxes, however.

English newspapers are available just about everywhere. Some are translated editions of local news publications, while others are Western magazines and newspapers that can be found on newsstands in the West.

Radio programs broadcast in English can be heard on certain stations. Ask hotel staff or company personnel how to access these. Some television programming in English can be found in some locations, as well. These will vary from one country to the next, and you cannot expect to find English-speaking programs in every area, so be sure to ask.

Internet Use

Internet access can be found in hotels and organizations. In addition, there are Internet hook-ups at Internet cafes around the larger cities for convenience. An hour of Web browsing in Saudi Arabia, for example, costs SR3 to SR10. Internet cards for connecting your computer can be purchased for ten hours at SR10 from quality companies like Awal Net, Nesma, and Saudi Net. Computer shops sell cards, as do Jarir Bookstores and certain stationery shops. Keep in mind the Internet is supervised, with at least 2,000 blocked sites, most of which are adult pornography, but also include some political, health, and educational sites. A complete list of censorship rules and forbidden topics for each country can be found at www.al-bab.com/media/freedom.htm. Use caution about the material you access, receive, or send to others in or out of the countries, due to active censorship processes.

Successful Presentations

Arab clients will be impressed by presentations that are sharp and use the latest technology. Making the effort for a sharp presentation and arranging for the proper equipment will pay off.

During your presentation, respect the hierarchy and focus on the senior man present. The presenter should also be the equivalent rank as the senior Arab present. Also ensure that your graphics are printed right to left so they are interpreted correctly. Since this is the way Arabs read, this is how they will interpret your graphics.[1]

The introduction is the most important part of your presentation. Within the opening few minutes you must catch their attention, therefore, do not begin with background information. Begin with the advantages of your product and the obvious benefits to them. A good introduction will take much preparation and research on the target organization.[2] It is also wise to provide prospective clients with literature in Arabic, especially if you expect them to pass it on to their customers.

Technology

While Internet access is becoming widely available throughout the Arabian Peninsula, laptop hook-ups are still somewhat complicated. The power supply voltage is different from that in other countries, so you have to be careful not to risk hurting your equipment. Bring a universal AC adaptor that lets you plug in wherever you like without damage. Plug adaptors for each country also will be needed. See Appendix E for Web sites where you can find voltage and plug information for each country.

You also will want to purchase a global modem or a local PC-card modem for a particular country where you plan to spend a considerable amount of time.

Telephone sockets can vary from one place to another, so it is a good idea to have a U.S. RJ-11 telephone adaptor for the modem.

The telephone companies function as servers and provide Internet access. It's a good idea to open an Internet account with a global ISP such as AOL, unless you plan to visit public access points to check email. You will need to bring your incoming mail (POP or IMAP) server name, your account name, and your password. You might want to take advantage of free Web email programs like Yahoo or Hotmail. Be prepared to wait for slow connection speeds or congested user areas at public Internet access areas.

For more information about traveling with a laptop or a palm computer, you can visit www.teleadapt.com or www.roadwarriortips.com.

Quote Requests

Quote requests may be negotiated somewhat differently than what you are accustomed to in other parts of the world. Shrewd traders, your Arab hosts may offer rationales like those that follow to angle for a better price:

- This is the first order, and thus a trial basis for future business.
- The first order will provide a test opportunity to see how the product fares in the local market. The accompanying risk thus deserves a price break.
- Another overseas supplier has quoted a better price.
- Local suppliers can provide the same merchandise at similar cost, or slightly higher. The Arab negotiator may appear willing to pay a slightly higher cost from a local supplier for the advantage of faster delivery time and shipping facilitation.
- Your quote, along with shipping and taxes, will prevent the resale locally for a decent profit margin, or will prove too competitive to gain a sizable edge in the marketplace.
- A better price for a first order may lead to larger orders in the future.
- You may be asked to quote a price for a substantial quantity of items, and thus bid lower, only to receive a smaller order that is expected to be paid at the lesser cost that was bid for a larger order.

However, these conditions actually may apply in certain cases, so keep that in mind as the negotiations continue. Here are some tips that can help you deal with the quote requests in a fair and balanced manner:

- Stay calm and enjoy the process! Remember that haggling is a recreational sport as much as a business procedure. The practice is common and expected.

- Avoid giving your lowest and best pricing up front, even if the hypothetical order is allegedly large. Quantities can change as negotiations continue, so start a bit high and work your way down through the negotiating process until you officially determine the actual number of units and order size. This will help you get a good price for your company as well as give your Arab client a fair price or discount after detailed negotiations.
- Research your product's market, availability, and local pricing to determine a win-win position for your quote.
- Base each quote on a quantity or unit price. This strategy provides latitude for current negotiations and offers a range for future orders.[3]

Specific fees and conditions will need to be spelled out verbally before putting the order in writing. Be sure to have copies made in Arabic as well as in your native language, and that all parties have clear understanding of the contents of each document.

Letters of Credit

Securing a letter of credit is an important part of doing business on the Arabian Peninsula. Frequently offered for a first-time order from a foreign supplier, letters of credit are secure means of payment for both parties. After you are awarded a contract, your customer will probably open a letter of credit in favor or your company.

Furthermore, if an Arab company is involved in a deal for which the government is the recipient of goods or services, the company cannot be paid by the government until delivery, after which payment may be made one or two months later. Thus, some companies prefer dealing with banks to manage payments.

U.S. banks may be unwilling to accept an Arab company's letter of credit. A back-to-back letter of credit might be needed in the event the original bank lacks the fiscal resources to cover the order. Sometimes the original bank prefers the back-to-back method to avoid tying their funds to exports.

A possible solution is to work with U.S.-Arabian banks, which often are willing to collaborate in deals of this type.

Payments typically do not follow the pattern laid out in the agreement and are often late. There are many possible causes for this, but if a government ministry is involved, your commission agent should get involved to sort it out for you. You should anticipate late payments of up to several months and include the cost of money in your price.

Marketing

As you plan a marketing campaign to launch your product in the Arab market, you will want to keep several guidelines in mind, as this market is quite different from those in the West.

Marketing literature should be reproduced in quality Arabic translation. If possible, work with a translator inside the country where the product is being launched rather than one that resides elsewhere. Don't expect or request a word-for-word translation, as this can compromise message integrity and meaning, and may unintentionally cross social boundaries or conflict with culture. Be certain that the text does not contain confusing or offensive material.

Maintain a conservative image for your product. Avoid sexual, religious, or political symbols, overtones, and themes. Don't compare two brands of the same product. Instead, focus on the value of your product in a stand-alone approach.

The primary marketing outlets are newspapers, magazines, and television.[4] Telemarketing is considered to be an invasion of privacy and is not really used in Arab regions. Advertising and marketing firms are beginning to operate more on the peninsula, but they lack consistent industry guidelines and regulations.

Marketing research with respect to the Middle East may prove fruitful in preparing your product for the public. It's better to take extra time to market your product appropriately than to launch it with inadequate preparation that may leave you with an impaired business reputation.

Friendships and Business

A successful business enterprise in the Arabian Peninsula requires social as well as professional connections. Although you may prefer to simply jet in, make the deal, and jet out again, that is not how business is conducted in Arabian Peninsula countries. Your Arab associates will want to get to know you, build trust and respect of your character, and develop a friendship that transcends the business experience.

Complying with this model can be aided by the following steps:

1. Study the culture, history, and people before you go. The more you understand beforehand, the better you can deal with situations as they arise during your visit. Trying to visit an Arab country "blind" and unprepared is likely to lead to frustration and dissatisfaction on both sides.

2. Become familiar with the business culture of your client's company, their products, needs, and terms. You might try the SWOT approach: strengths, weaknesses, opportunities, and threats of doing business with this particular country or client. Also learn the government and industry rules that regulate negotiations.

3. Invest in personal friendships as much as professional associations. With little effort you can readily learn to admire, respect, and enjoy the people that will receive you warmly and enthusiastically. There will be much to see and do, and your Arab hosts will do everything in their power to ensure that you have a pleasurable experience. Take a reciprocal approach by providing helpful information they may desire, such as the best vacation spots, restaurants, or schools in your homeland or places you have visited.

4. Respect Arab expertise and experience. After all, you are negotiating for a share of their market, not yours, so adopt a two-way communication policy that invites opinions and suggestions from your Arab associates.

5. Don't overlook the need for long-term relations for future orders. Build recognition with periodic follow-up and reminders of your products and services. A friendly social call is a great way to build camaraderie and longevity. Be available for advice and assistance, and in time, your business connection may bear fruit.

6. Provide agent support. Build a relationship with your agent(s) to keep them in tune with your company's goals and to offset any difficulties they may encounter. If feasible, place a home com-

pany representative alongside the agent for training and support. Occasional telephone calls, training seminars, and product updates allows you to help your agent(s) do the best possible job with your products.[5]

Doing business in Arabian Peninsula countries should be an enjoyable experience, built over time, rather than a quick rush of activity followed by a flat-line response.

Who to Send on the Trip

If you plan to send a company representative to conduct business with an Arab company in the peninsula, or if you have begun the process on-site, returned home, and now want to send a representative in a supervisory or follow-up capacity, you will need to choose the right person and prepare him accordingly.

First, it is advisable to send a man, not a woman. As discussed previously, women business representatives are not well received in Arab countries. If they are dressed appropriately and behave conservatively, they still may be viewed as curiosities rather than as authorities, and at worst, may be treated ill by some Arab men who consider the women out of their element. If you must send a woman, make sure she understands Arab culture and protocol. But your interests will be better served if you send one or more men, likewise familiar with the culture, to handle negotiations. Married men who travel with their wives to Saudi Arabia should plan to accompany them in public, as women are not allowed to appear with a man who is not a male relative or husband. However, married spouses do not show affection for each other when people are around to see.

Your representative(s) should dress conservatively in public, and usually also in private, except in private housing compounds for expatriates or at beaches with other Westerners. This means no shorts, and preferably no short sleeves. Men do not have to adopt the Arab mode of dress, but they are expected to cover themselves in modest fashion.

Business behavior and public conduct require a quiet manner, or at least one that does not draw attention due to raucous laughing, joking, arguing, etc.

The person you send should have some background in Arab culture and customs. Hopefully, he has experience or familiarity with the business environment into which he is traveling. He may have worked with Arabs before and has some idea of how to proceed with Arab clients now. He may also know a few Arabic expressions.

Your company's representative should be patient, trustworthy, and authoritative in the sense that he demonstrates confidence, not arrogance. He will have an understanding of how negotiations proceed in Arab culture, and what to do when unexpected things happen. He should be the kind of person that others respect and admire, and who knows how to get things done without ruffling feathers. He can identify opportunities and take appropriate action to facilitate processes.

Provide the best possible preparation for the person you plan to send, including possible language classes, culture seminars, and practice negotiations at home to ensure the best chance of success.

Connecting to the Arab Market

In many respects doing business in your home country and doing business on the Arabian Peninsula is similar: finding a market niche, arousing consumer interest, and making your product available to the satisfaction of both buyer and seller.

But in other important ways, launching your product in the Arab market requires a significant amount of planning and adjusting your market strategy. In addition to cross-cultural considerations like language, government, and purchasing trends, a Western businessperson must make suitable connections that will lead to lucrative sales. These connections are all-important to the success of a marketing plan.

1. Business and social crossover relationships should be sought. Make an effort to locate Arab companies, agents, and marketers with whom you feel comfortable doing business. They should be persons of integrity with reputations for quality performance and proven experience.
2. Demonstrate good character in your business transactions. Maintaining a positive image will help to attract the highest quality companies and people with whom to build business relationships.

3. Cultivate a proactive attitude toward your clients and the community. A friendly attitude and warm demeanor are inviting to professional associates and potential clients. Obviously, you shouldn't overdo it and retain some reserve, but you will be perceived as a welcome addition to the Arab marketplace with a display of good nature and fair play.
4. Develop interests in other topics besides business. Be ready to chat about the environment, current news, local events, architecture, science, or other interests that will provide opportunities to compare ideas and exchange perspectives in entertaining dialogue. Become a well-rounded addition to the community.
5. Make it easy for your clients to do business with you. High service standards are at a premium everywhere in the world. All of us like to shop where we feel welcome and valued by competent professionals. Assess your business process periodically to clear out the bugs, and seek client feedback so you can address their concerns and problems.
6. Stay in touch. After making initial contact with potential clients, don't give up on those who take their time in placing an order. Establish brand recognition and be gently persistent. Also, make a point of checking in after a sale, when feasible, to ensure the client is satisfied and to deal with any questions that might come up. Your responsible attitude will be appreciated.

Delving deep into Arab culture will lead you to pearls of adventure and success. You just have to be willing to dive in and perform the right moves to find your hidden treasure.

Establishing Compliance

Establishing a meaningful relationship with local agents is an integral part of doing business on the Arabian Peninsula by adhering to local laws and following established protocols. In addition to checking credentials and keeping the channels of communication open as discussed in a previous chapter, it also is important to pay attention to the day-to-day details that comprise a productive business association. Taking time to do this will enhance the overall relationship between your agent and you, and ultimately benefit your company and the market by the quality of service and products that you are able to provide.

Make sure that your agent and you share the same business philosophy. If you do not, you probably will be unable to work together for long. This kind of understanding should be reached at the pre-hiring level through the questions you ask, along with resulting discussion, which will reveal your attitudes to each other. If your agent's views differ markedly from yours in some ways, ascertain whether he is willing to do things your way, and if he can be trusted to do so. Failure in this area could result in serious legal breaches or contractual problems.

Set up a communications system on a regular basis. You may want to arrange telephone check-ins, email contacts, or other informal meetings where you are available to answer questions, make decisions, and supply guidance. Otherwise, your agent may feel he has to fend for himself and eventually lose interest in or be unable to perform a good job for your company.

Continue to strengthen the relationship with your agent. Let him know you care about him as a person, not just as a subordinate or mere business associate. When appropriate, share meals and engage in casual conversations. Get his opinions on how to handle delicate matters or a change in plans. Encourage him to feel like a valuable contributor to the overall business plan.

Coordinate a record-keeping system that organizes information and makes it readily accessible to your agent and others who may need it. Keep accurate records with a clear paper trail (even an electronic one) in case your company or agent is questioned by the government or client and records are summoned.

A skilled agent can make the difference between a successful enterprise and a failed one. Do whatever you can to find the right agent for the job, and then switch your focus to keeping him on board.

Using Interpreters

Like language translators with written documents, interpreters play a vital role in exchanging oral information between interested parties in business negotiations. Although your client may offer to provide an interpreter for you – and this is acceptable if you cannot find one yourself – it may be better to hire one on your own to ensure that the person has the necessary skills to communicate effectively and to ensure terms, conditions, and perceptions are translated and interpreted as you expect. This is especially important due to the vagueness of the language.

Arabic fluency is a good starting point, but other considerations should be taken into account when hiring an interpreter:

- Level of proficiency
- Amount and type of experience
- Accent, dialect, vocabulary distinctions among various Arab regions
- Accuracy vs. eloquence vs. literal interpretation
- References
- Potential personal interests or biases
- Availability

A good interpreter is indispensable and may be able to advise you on matters of social protocol or communicative uncertainties. Good people skills and a pleasant manner are helpful, too.

As can be seen in this chapter, how you say something is as important as what you say. Finding the right resources to facilitate communication is one of the first things you will want to do when planning your foray into the Arab business world.

Chapter Six

The Arab Way

Engaging in international business requires additional effort beyond professional skills and industry knowledge. You will need to understand the social context of your enterprise as well as the way that people live, and how your business might impact their lives.

This chapter explores the human side of doing business on the Arabian Peninsula. Although much of the following information can change from one country to another, the topics below provide insight to Arab culture overall so that you may become better prepared to visit and perhaps establish commercial roots in this fascinating neighborhood of the global community.

Names and Titles

People are named in ways that are both similar to and different from Western naming traditions. Some families name children after older or deceased relatives, just as we do in the West. However, you do not address people by their title and surname (family name). Only first names are used. The second name is the father's name, and the third name is the grandfather's name. These are followed by the family name, usually beginning with *Al* (the), and sometimes a tribal identification. Westerners should use just first names when addressing Arabs, and expect to be called by their first name, in return. If the person has a title, it should be used with the first name, for example Major John, Doctor Debra, or Sheikh Ali (Ali being the first name). Women do not change their names when they marry and should also be called by their first names. It is important to find out if a person has a title, not using a title could be an insult.

For "Mr.," you should use *sayyed* (which means 'sir'), and for women, *sayeeda*. *Sayyed* or *sharif* are also used for descendents of the Prophet Mohammad.

The titles *Sheikh* (or *Shaikh*) and *Amir* (or *Emir*) are used differently in peninsula countries. In Saudi Arabia, the head of state has the title *King* and male members of the royal family take the designation, "*Amir*" (prince). In Bahrain, the ruler also now has the title King but members of the royal family have the title *Sheikh*. In Kuwait and Qatar, the ruler is called *Amir* and members of the royal family *Sheikh*. In Oman, the ruler has the title *Sultan* and male members of royal family are referred to as *Sayyed*. In the UAE the head of state has the title *Sheikh*.

In Saudi Arabia, the term *Shiekh* can also be a mark of respect for senior businessmen, high-ranking government officials, and older males that are not relatives.[1] *Shiekh* can also refer to religious scholars or the head of a tribe. Female members of royal families are termed *Sheikha* or *Shaikha* with the female form used rarely in Saudi Arabia. Few non-peninsula Arabs have the male or female title.

Another common title is *Hajji*. This is someone who has performed the pilgrimage. Also when the first son is born the father may be called *Abu* (father) and the mother *Umm* (mother), followed by the name of the son. Some people will also use *ibn* (son of) or *bint* (daughter of) before the ancestral name. Since the use of an Arab's first name does not indicate any informal status or close relationship as it does in the West, substitutes such as *Hajji, Abu, Umm, ibn,* and *bint* are adopted to indicate informality.

People may have several names for legal purposes but will omit some of them in daily use. It is not unusual for members of the same family to have different combinations of names. People are also not always consistent when using their names. Because the first name is the only name that is consistent, some Arab countries list names in the phone directory by first name and some companies keep records by first names. However, on the peninsula most phone directories list by family name.[2]

Dress

Generally, inhabitants of the Arabian Peninsula countries dress modestly as prescribed by the Qur'an. Men wear a loose head covering, called a *gutra*. Often, this is a white cloth, but in Saudi Arabia, men wear red-and-white checked fabric. A black head rope to secure the *gu-tra* is called an *agal*.

In Qatar and parts of the UAE, some men add to their headgear with two cords strung from the *agal* for decorous purposes. Citizens of Oman, Yemen, and southern Saudi Arabia frequently don a turban that is wound about their heads. The Omanis decorate these with colorful embroidery about the edges.

Males in the peninsula wear a floor-length robe, or shirt-dress, called a *thobe* in Saudi Arabia, Bahrain, and Qatar. In the Kuwait, UAE, and Oman, it is a *dishdasha*.

For women, the black, flowing gown seen in most media images is called the *abeyya*. The accompanying *burqa*, or veil, comes in four types: thin gauze to cover the face, a veil that covers the face but not the eyes, a mask hiding the nose, cheeks, and part of the mouth, or a basic headscarf (*hijaab*) that hides the hair and neck. However, in Bahrain and Kuwait, more and more women are shedding the veil and headscarf.[3]

Foreign visitors to the Arabian Peninsula do not have to adopt Arab dress, but they should plan to wear modest, conservative fashions to avoid problems. Violating the dress code can lead to legal charges and penalties if you are cited by the Committee for the Propagation of Virtue and Prevention of Vice, otherwise known as the *mutawwa*, or religious police force in Saudi Arabia. Western businessmen are expected to attend business meetings in a business suit, despite the hot weather. Not wearing a suit can be insulting to your host. Western women may wear an *abeyya* to conform with the rules for modest dress; however, Western men should not wear the traditional Arab robes. These robes have taken on nationalistic meanings and the wearing of one by an outsider may be considered mocking.

Religion

Islam is the prevailing faith throughout much of the Middle East and it is impossible to establish business relationships without some understanding of it. In the Arabian Peninsula, Islam governs not only people's spiritual beliefs and public worship, but also their personal lives and business behavior, with laws that legislate moral behavior to conform to lifestyle teachings in the Qur'an. Care must be taken to re-spect Islamic customs in behavior, dress, and language. No matter your religious beliefs, even if you have none at all, you should plan to follow the prescribed code of conduct as modeled by your Arab hosts and as-sociates. If in doubt, check with an Islamic expert. Because the religion is so complex, it is also advisable that you do some research on your own about Islam before doing business in the region.

The religion of Islam began in the seventh century with the birth of the Prophet Mohammed in AD 570 in the city of Mecca, located in modern Saudi Arabia. The Qur'an teaches that the Prophet received spiritual insight from Allah, delivered by the archangel Gabriel. The Qur'an recorded these teachings later in *suras*, or verses.

Islam means submission. The religion teaches that Allah, or God, determines all events, and that humans are subject to his will. Visitors to the region frequently hear expressions like *inshallah* (if God wills it) with respect to the future, and *al-hamdu lillah* (thanks be to God), which extends gratitude for common and unique blessings.

The Qur'an is believed to report God's exact words, not representa-tions from prophets or visionaries. It has retained the same basic form since its inception. Interestingly, the Qur'an makes many references to beliefs and people renowned in Judaism and Christianity, i.e., Abra-ham, Jesus, and Mary, the mother of Jesus.

The Five Pillars of faith are as follows:

1. ***Shahada***. This is a declaration of faith stating that only Allah is the one, true God: "There is no God but the God and Mohammed is his Prophet," which must be stated publicly. It can be heard in the public call to prayers that echoes throughout the cities.
2. ***Salat***. Muslims must pray five times daily—sunrise, noon, mid-afternoon, sunset, and night. They can pray in public places or private homes, except on Friday at noon, during which believers pray at a mosque, if possible. Before praying, adherents must perform the ablution of washing their arms, hands, feet, and head to symbolize their humility and submission to God. In lieu of water (in dusty or outlying places), dust or sand can be sym-bolically used. Muslims pray facing the shrine of *Kaaba* in Mecca. Some public buildings display arrows pointing to the correct prayer direction.

3. *Zakat.* Alms-giving is based on $1/40^{th}$ (2.5%) of a person's annual income and is collected for redistribution to those in poorer straits. Today the system operates as a social welfare service, not just a religious contribution, for supporting mosques and religious charitable organizations.

4. **Fast of Ramadan**. In AD 610 the Prophet Mohammed received his first revelation in the month of Ramadan. Each year, Muslims commemorate this event by fasting from sunrise to sunset during the month, and by abstaining from taking things into their bodies, such as food, drink, sexual activity, or smoking during daylight hours. Only children, the infirm, and travelers are excused. During the ninth month of the Muslim calendar, restaurants are open fewer hours during the day, and prohibitions increase, so be extra cautious when traveling to the peninsula at this time. Business hours are generally reduced during Ramadan, so try to avoid doing business during the month.

5. **Pilgrimage or *Hajj* to Mecca.** At least once in their lifetime, every Muslim who is able must make a pilgrimage to Mecca in Saudi Arabia. Muslims from all over the world meet there as one community living their faith. The trip requires a sacrifice of time, status, and comfort. The *hajj* season follows Ramadan.

The manifestation of these principals are evident everywhere so it is important to note their importance.

The Sunni and Shiite denominations evolved following the Prophet Mohammed's death in AD 632. The Shiites (partisans) followed Ali bin Abi Taleb, Mohammed's cousin and son-in-law, as successor, while the Sunni elected to follow Abu Bakr, the Prophet's close friend and father-in-law; the latter was confirmed as chosen leader in two subsequent competitions. As a result, although Ali ruled briefly as the fourth *caliph*, he was assassinated. His line of followers, the Shiites, hold fast to the spiritual authority of the *imams*. In actuality, both groups follow similar teachings and practice similar beliefs.

Except for Saudi Arabia, Roman Catholic and Protestant churches can be found in all countries, mainly in the capital cities. Bahrain and Yemen also have synagogues. Check your guidebook for locations and service times.

Eids (Holidays)

Eids are holidays or special celebrations, usually of religious (Islamic) origin. The Islamic New Year is called *Ras as-Sana*. The *Shia* holiday of *Ashura* is the anniversary of the martyring of Hussein, who was the third Shiite imam. The Prophet's birthday is called *Moulid an-Nabi*, or feast of the Prophet. Ramadan is discussed above.

Since each country celebrates these *Eids* in their own way, it is best to check with your Arab friends to see what the locals are doing before making plans. Many festivals center on feasting and visiting, with a day off from work, and these make for an enjoyable or reflective time. Also the dates change each year due to the lunar calendar, so it is best to check before you depart to see if any of the dates fall during your trip. Some governments will extend the two main *Eids* sometimes, so it is best to avoid scheduling a business trip near them. See Appendix E for a Web site where you can find the dates for holidays for each country.

The two main E*ids* are *al-Fitr* and *al-Adha*. The E*id al-Fitr* opens the celebration indicating the end of the Ramadan fast; it is joyful and light-hearted, often compared to the Christian Christmas. The *Eid al-Adha* is the period that marks the end of the pilgrimage to Mecca. Even if you do not join these festivities, be careful not to do anything that will offend your hosts that do celebrate them.

You may wish to send an *Eid* card a few days before the commencement of festivities to Arab associates and friends that you know well. In return, they might send you a thank-you card.

Marriages

Courtships and marriages typically are arranged in traditional Arab families. You are not free to date or court an Arab woman for romance or marriage, unless her family has specifically approved it. By law, Muslim women cannot marry non-Muslims, but Muslim men are able to wed Jewish or Christian women if they convert to Islam, but not Buddhists or Hindus.

The courtship may be settled by the parents before the couple knows each other well, or at all. There may be an official arrangement for the pair to become acquainted or even to get engaged. But even following such an arrangement, with papers signed and gifts exchanged, the couple will not be left alone until they are married. They must be chaperoned by responsible family members who will enforce moral conduct. If a couple should be found alone together or be caught in a promiscuous situation, there will be a scandal, and one family may bring charges against the other. The woman's reputation may be tarnished, the arrange relationship broken, and her shame will rebound on her family in this communal-style culture.

Conversely, weddings are lavish affairs and may have a modern flair or a traditional theme. Bride and groom are kept separate leading up to the wedding day, when the groom comes to claim his bride. Music, segregated dancing, and feasting make for great fun at these weddings. Men and women traditionally have separate receptions in large wedding halls or hotels. Bedouin wedding parties are held in huge tents decorated with lights. If you are invited, you are sure to enjoy it.

Recreation

Try to visit one of the mosques, called the *masjid*, or *jamaa*, while you are there. Though some can be simple edifices with basic decorations, others are magnificent representations of Islamic architecture and faith. There you can admire the tiles, paneling, and wood-carved designs, many of which are centuries old. Guests are usually welcome to visit, as long as they are modestly dressed and do not arrive during the Friday noon prayers. Expect to remove your shoes; for a small fee, some mosques provide temporary indoor footwear.

The Arabian Peninsula landscape is timeless and breath taking. A sizable desert, called the Empty Quarter, comprises about 25% of the region. You may want to schedule a tour with an experienced guide to view the sand dunes, oases, plains, and salt flats. Two mountain ranges will compete for your attention: the Haraz Mountains in Yemen, and the Jabal Akhdar mountains of Oman. The Red Sea, Arabian Sea, and Arabian Gulf (known as the Persian Gulf in the West) surround the peninsula. Desert outings can be arranged by a tour company or through your hotel. Many tour companies offer "*wadi* bashing" in an SUV followed by a meal and entertainment at a "Bedouin camp." These are enjoyed by tourists and locals alike and are well worth the price. Many water sports are available at various resorts and harbors along the coast.

Wildlife of old included an exciting array of beasts, such as cheetahs, leopards, wolves, and hyenas. Most of these are extinct or nearly so, which means you'll have to turn your watchful eyes toward smaller exotic creatures like sand rats, lizards, and the less common scorpion or snake. Rare (in the West) birds, sea creatures, and plant life can be spotted with the aid of an experienced guide. Wildlife sanctuaries and national parks have begun to organize, with more scheduled for the future. Check with your hosts to find out if one is located near you.

Resorts offer plenty of fascinating activities, like boat rides and theme park-type attractions for the kids. Sports like horseback riding, bowling, cricket, and soccer are available, along with go-karts, tennis, fishing, golf, and ice-skating. Cave exploring (with appropriate preparations and cautions), bicycling, and diving or snorkeling are among popular pastimes favored by visitors and tourists. Some cities boast performing arts programs like opera and ballet by regional or visiting troupes.

Camel races and horse races are plentiful, especially during the winter and spring; many offer free admission – but betting is not allowed.

All countries also have excellent museums that you will want to visit, especially the National Museum of Dubai in Al Fahidi Fort. It is located along the creek on the Bur Dubai side.

Shopping

Whether you are looking for decorative items to brighten your office in the peninsula, or shopping for artisan wares or cultural souvenirs, be sure to check out the fine arts boutiques and shops. Although religious scholars believe the Qur'an is against depictions of the human body, artists have created beautiful designs from geometric shapes and flora that adorn everything from books to buildings. Calligraphy is another striking manifestation of art, using Arabic letters in decorative script.

Woven rugs, tapestries, wall hangings, and table covers, along with clothing and even Bedouin tents are not to be missed. Everyone has heard of Persian and Turkish carpets, and with good reason. But the peninsula has a fair number of gifted weavers whose wares can be viewed in museums and purchased around town, especially in the *souqs* (or *suqs*), meaning markets, and the bazaars, where you can find numerous styles of art and designs at competitive prices. Look for rugs (*kilims*), pearls, embroidered cotton clothes, Bedouin woven bags, decorated daggers and swords, copper and brass products, olive and cedar woodcarving, water pipes, cushion covers, frankincense and incense, and gold jewelry as well as fine Bedouin silver jewelry.[4] Many stores feature the latest designs from Paris and Rome, while others offer homogenous designs made by hand. You will find a vast assortment of things to choose from for yourself or as a gift for someone else. Remember to use your bargaining skills to get the highest quality at the best price; the seller expects it and has priced his wares accordingly.

In addition to shops and the bazaar, you also can find supermarkets that often sell imports from countries around the world. Prices can be high, but it is still possible to bargain, so offer a lower price than is asked, starting at about 30%. Go up from there as necessary until you either purchase the item at your price or decide to pass.

Hospitality

If you are in the position to offer hospitality while living in the Arabian Peninsula, it's a good idea to do so. Not only will you have the chance to develop friendly relationships in your new environment, but also you will be able to get accustomed to the culture and secure a social niche in the business community as well as in your personal life.

You don't have to entertain lavishly. A home-cooked meal or a restaurant dinner provides a hospitable treat for your guests. It is helpful for you to become familiar with coffee rituals and preferred beverages, like coffee and tea, rather than soda.

Do not offer alcohol to your guests unless you are sure they drink it. Also store alcohol in your home out-of-sight, some Muslims are offended by the mere sight of alcohol.

At dinner or over coffee, be sure to ply your guests with several invitations to partake. It is customary for them to refuse the first or second offer, but to accept thereafter. The same holds true for you. It is all right to refuse the first invitation to have coffee or stay and dine, but then feel free to accept.

Invitations

If you are invited to dine with an Arab associate, do not assume the invitation extends to your wife or other female relative that may be with you. Plan to attend alone unless your host specifically indicates otherwise.

Similarly, do not assume your Arab guest will bring his wife when invited to dine or visit with you. Unless the couple is quite Westernized and the group will be gathering at a hotel function with other Westernized couples, it is unlikely an Arab wife will accompany her husband.

Visiting Homes

Arabs are friendly people, and they enjoy the opportunity of hosting guests in their homes. You are likely to receive an invitation to visit or dine with an Arab family, so consider it a great honor and mark of trust.

When you enter the home, shake hands with everyone to whom you are introduced, followed by the gesture of touching your heart with the palm of your right hand. For women, do not attempt to shake their hands unless they offer theirs first. Some Muslim men are uncomfortable touching a woman of any nationality, but this should not be considered an offense. Neither approach nor touch a woman unless she comes to you first, as some Westernized women may do. Try to learn an Arab greeting for in-person visitors (or telephone calls). Stand up when anyone other than a servant enters the room.

Ask about the person's health, and in general, the family. Do not inquire specifically about wives, daughters, or sisters – in fact, any female member – as this is considered inappropriate.

The coffee-drinking custom is to accept from one to three cups from your host, but to drink no more unless your host and other guests do. To signal your readiness for the second and third cup, hold out your small, handle-less cup toward the person doing the pouring. Hold the cup with your right hand. To show you have had enough, give your cup a brief twist.

Guests may be offered fresh fruit instead of or in addition to hot coffee or tea, along with a serving plate and paring utensil. Occasionally, pastries, chocolates, or cookies may be provided.

Guests are free to leave following coffee, which is served after dinner. Aside from a verbal thank-you, no follow-up note or phone call of gratitude will be made. Nor should you feel compelled to offer one afterwards if you are the guest. Keep in mind that being entertained at home is considered an honor reserved for those whom your Arab hosts want to know better. Begin your visit on a social note, and you may find that it will take a business turn before the end of your time together.

Hosts will see their guests to the door when it's time to depart, or even to the end of the drive or compound entrance. This courtesy dates back to tribal days when a host escorted a guest to the border of his territory in an effort to secure safe travel.

The *Majlis*

The *majlis* is a room in Arab houses reserved for male visitors, usually with a separate entrance. In Kuwait they are called *diwaniyahs*. The men will have regular gatherings there with friends and relatives. It is a chance to socialize and discuss politics, news, sports, or business. If you are invited to a *majlis*, it will be an enjoyable experience. It is an opportunity to get to know your counterpart and possibly discuss some business.

Majlis gatherings usually take place after the nightfall prayers. You are not expected to bring gifts or food. When you arrive do not approach too quickly, give them time to know you are coming. Do not be surprised if they seem to ignore you until you greet them. This is to give you time to remove your shoes and get organized. After removing your shoes, enter the room and say *as salam aleikum*. They will respond by saying *wa aleikum salam* and stand. Greet the host first then shake hands with everyone, starting on the right, in a counter-clockwise direction. You will probably be offered a seat next to the host, especially if you are a senior official or first-time visitor. If you are, offer your seat to the next visitor. If you are not offered, take a seat on the end. As you greet everyone be sure to look them in the eye. In a large *majlis*, everyone may not stand at once but will rise to meet you as you pass. After you sit down, men will shout greetings to you such as *"al-lah bilkheir"* (God make your evening good). You are now part of the *majlis* and should greet visitors the same way. Tea and coffee will be served and maybe a light meal. Your visit should take about 30 minutes, longer for meals. When you are ready to leave you just say *"ma salama"* and wave your hand to indicate it applies to everyone.

Dining

Whether dining out or cooking in, you will want to be aware of your menu options in the peninsula. Of course, at home you can cook whatever you like, providing the ingredients are available. At the major hotels, you typically can order a wide variety of Western dishes. But if you want to eat "Arab style," you can choose from three main types of cuisine.

The traditional "Arab" cuisine is actually Lebanese food, found virtually everywhere. This usually takes the form of a sizable choice of hot and cold appetizers, called *mezze*. Salads, bean dishes, lamb pies or sausages, and stews made with ingredients like lentils are among the many favorites, along with shish kebab and rice.

Another variation of food offerings is Southern Asian cuisine, which also may be found just about anywhere in the peninsula.

The third type is a little harder to find, and unique: Bedouin food, which includes *kebsa*, an entire lamb stuffed with rice and pine nuts.

Seasonings include coriander, cumin, cinnamon, nutmeg, ginger, turmeric, dill, and saffron. Bread comes with most meals, baked fresh at home or purchased from neighborhood bakeries.

Arab businessmen will often invite their foreign business associates to their homes for dinner. These dinners usually begin after the last prayer of the day and are therefore much later than you may be used to. In most homes, guests are first invited into the *majlis* for coffee and await other guests' arrival or for the meal preparations to be concluded. This pre-meal period is used to get to know each other. Stories are told, news exchanged, and business is discussed. The meal might be laid out in a nearby room or occasionally in the courtyard. A traditional meal is served from a common dish without cutlery and comprises one or more sheep arranged on platters of rice. Alternatively, fish may be served, and more rarely, a young camel. Although the meal might be set on a table, it is more often laid out on the floor. If many guests are present, they will eat in waves, so hold back unless the host urges you to eat as one of the principal group members. Sitting cross-legged or in a semi-kneeling position is the rule, as long as the sole of the foot is not indicated toward someone there.

Upon being seated, your host may begin the meal by saying *bismillaah*, which means "In the name of God," and start eating small amounts of rice. It is good for guests to follow suit and not appear too hurried. Many people use bread to sop moist or soupy items.

Note the following practices in visiting Arab homes for a meal:

1. Bringing a gift to the home is not required, but if you choose to do so, flowers or chocolates are good choices. In outlying areas, take fruit or honey.
2. Wash your hands before dining.
3. Eat with your right hand; keep the left hand out of sight, usually in your lap or under the table.
4. Serve yourself food from the side of the plate that faces you. Reaching toward another side of the platter is rude.
5. If offered the best of the meal by your host, accept it graciously as an honor.
6. Try to eat a little of everything.
7. Meat or the main part of the meal often is held until last, so don't rush for it.
8. Some people pick their teeth after a meal, using toothpicks.
9. Leaving a bit of residual food on your plate is a courteous way to show that you really are satisfied and full. You do not have to eat everything put in front of you.
10. As you finish eating and some begin to lick their fingers, guests will stand up and say "*alhamdillah*" (Praise be to God) and "*kaththar allah kheirkum*" (God increase your bounty) as a tribute to the host's generosity. Then guests are directed to a wash-up area for their hands, either a place of sinks or a bowl of soapy water with a rinse pitcher. Afterward, you will be taken back to the *majlis* area for coffee or tea.
11. Wait until coffee is served after a meal before leaving. If possible, try to have at least one cup of the beverage.

An added custom is the bringing of *ud*, or incense, which is handed to each guest, who then holds it beneath the head cloth and wafts the smoke with the right hand, leaving a pleasant scent on the clothing. As this is done, it is time to get up, compliment the host's graciousness, and be on your way. Good manners are universal throughout most societies. If in doubt, follow your host's example.

Living Conditions

Upon your arrival in a peninsula country, you may need to find temporary accommodations until permanent housing can be arranged. Hotels of every kind can be found throughout the region, from low-cost hostels, which aren't known for cleanliness or privacy, to economy-priced rooms that tend to be located in the more questionable parts of town.

Quality and top-level hotels offer the full range of amenities, some with golf club memberships and quite-good food. Top-end hotels can be found in all major cities and booked on the Internet, however, prices are very high so they may not be suited for extended stays. Alcohol (for Westerners) is served at the mid- to top-range of hotels in bars and nightclubs, except Saudi Arabia, Kuwait, and Sharjah in the UAE. Many also have entertainment; some are very noisy.

Flats, villas, and hotel suites can be rented at all price levels. Check utility costs, as air conditioning may be priced in addition to electricity. The villas may include a garden, while apartment blocks often feature a common swimming pool and health club. A compound area, similar to a gated development in the West, sometimes has its own restaurant, shops, and park. Renting older homes is another option that can be less expensive than newer housing. In exchange for charm, you may have to sacrifice convenience.

You can find housing advertised in English language newspapers, at Embassies and cultural organizations, and in companies or among professional associates. Realtors and relocation consultants are listed in the telephone directory. There are also many Web sites that list accommodations for rent. See Appendix E for a partial list. Property ownership laws vary greatly from country to country and are rapidly changing. See Appendix E for where to find the latest laws and consult your Embassy or agent for updates.

Housing areas that are popular with visitors often are located near the city center, close to shopping areas, or within easy commuting distance to schools. International schools for Western children, especially for British and American students, are located in virtually all the larger cities. Those for French and German students are more limited.

For medical care, you can register with a private clinic, find a competent medic (many have been trained and licensed in the West), or go to a local hospital. Check with your regular doctor before leaving to see if vaccinations are recommended for the regions in which you will be staying.

In the rare event you should be arrested and charged with a criminal offense, telephone your embassy or consulate and wait for their representative to come before you make decisions or sign documents.

Western and Arab Women in Public

A Western wife who travels with her husband to the Arabian Peninsula should have no special concerns as long as she maintains a modest appearance and conservative attitude – the same as her husband should.

Females traveling alone may be more subject to scrutiny and curiosity. To avoid unwanted attention, keep the following in mind:

- Wearing a wedding ring will make you appear less "available."
- Give the impression you are traveling with a spouse or group.
- Wear sunglasses in public and avoid a direct gaze at men.
- Ignore crude comments and be aware of your surroundings in a crowd.
- On public transportation, try to sit next to a woman.
- Do not display a flirtatious attitude, which can be misinterpreted by Arab men.
- If someone affronts or follows you, go to the lobby of a large hotel or a major store; ask the clerk to call the police, if necessary.

Many Arab women hold professional jobs while married, even with children. They hold household authority in their homes and retain money in their own names that their husbands cannot control. Due to

Western films and media that depict loose morals among today's women, some Arab men view Western females as the opportunity to get around their country's moral code. Usually, verbal harassment is the worst women will receive.[5]

Local Transportation

In addition to local buses and taxis, many people get around on bicycles, even tourists, after they get used to the climate. Motorcycles are another option, though less common in the peninsula. There are no trains.

You can bring your own vehicle, but shipping and registration can be difficult. It probably is easiest to hire a local car or driver to get around town. Although fuel is cheap and plentiful in towns and cities, it can be hard to find a refueling station out in the open, so fill up whenever you get the chance. Diesel fuel is less readily available.

Garages or service centers can be found in many urban areas, except in Yemen. Check with your car's manufacturer ahead of time for information about locating spare parts if needed.

Road signs, parking meters, and traffic guards are becoming more apparent in most cities. You can drive on your own country's driver's license for a temporary period of one week to a month in most peninsula countries, but in Saudi Arabia with special permission, you may be able to use it for up to three months. After that, you will need to apply for an international driving permit, which requires the following special documentation – some, like Saudi Arabia, will want Arab-language translations:

- Valid national driver's permit (from home country)
- No-objection certificate from your employer (NOC)
- Accommodation rental contract
- Passport photocopies
- Passport-size photos
- Possible blood group certification

Rental cars are available from major companies like Hertz. Assess traffic conditions in your area, along with your driving competency, before making this choice, as minor and major accidents are common, and insurance is compulsory. In fact, Saudi Arabia and the UAE have some of the world's highest accident rates. In the event of an injury, you will be held accountable. Be wary of women pedestrians, as they tend to step out in front of vehicles unexpectedly.

You will need a travel permit in Yemen and Saudi Arabia, which can be obtained in those countries.

Seatbelts are required, but rarely enforced. Driving with hand-held mobile phones is illegal but common. If you plan on driving across desert terrain, take extra precautions like water supplies, light clothing for day and warm covers for night, flares for breakdowns, etc. Let someone know where you're going and when you'll return.

Tipping

Although it is common throughout the Middle East, in the Arabian Peninsula, tipping as practiced by Westerners is not widely done. However, taxi drivers, tourist guides, and other service personnel who arrange contracts with tourists or long-term visitors will expect tips, so plan accordingly.

Since restaurants often keep the service charge applied to the bill instead of giving it to the servers, leaving a small tip on the table for good service is greatly appreciated.

Personal Behavior & Questions

The first time you travel to the Arabian Peninsula, you may feel uncomfortable and out of place in your new surroundings. This is normal for any traveler in a new situation. The better prepared you are before departure, the easier that things will go. Know in advance who you can ask when you have questions. It may be a company executive stationed in the country, your company's agent, an embassy or consulate official, an Arab host, or another company's representative. Keep telephone numbers and addresses handy, carrying them in your wallet or purse when you go out each day.

Furthermore, it's a good idea to have a list of instructions for someone at the company, or a relative in your home country, with you in the event of your illness or an accident. Difficulties like these are hard enough in a familiar environment, but when you are abroad, they can be confusing, frustrating, and even frightening for someone to navigate.

In general, maintain a low profile and a pleasant demeanor. Show respect and courtesy, along with confidence and competence, to everyone with whom you come in contact. They will respect you in return, and most people are eager to help when they can.

Keep in mind that in public, people can be aggressive and rude, which is the cultural norm. In private, their manners are much more polite and considerate. It is acceptable for you to follow these models of behavior.

Preserving Honor

If you should make a mistake or find yourself in an awkward situation, be ready to apologize and make things right, but do so without losing face or causing your Arab associates to lose face. This is a vital concept in the region.

As discussed previously, Arabs will go out of their way to avoid hurting your feelings or telling you *no*. They will delay bad news and even seem to go along with the very thing they have no intention of accepting. They may expect similar behavior from you although they are familiar with Western business tactics, and may misinterpret your language or behavior if you fail to follow suit.

Avoid a defensive attitude and the need to be proven right. Do not try to force a sense of accountability on your Arab associates by "calling" them on what you perceive to be avoidance or unnecessary delays. Arabs have delicate self-esteem that is easily damaged by careless or overt criticism. When you must say something unpleasant to an Arab associate, try to do so without implying judgment. Criticizing an Arab, especially before others, is an affront to his honor and self-esteem.

Privacy

Privacy as we know it in the West is non-existent in Arab culture. While people do maintain individual or shared households in relative privacy from public observation, within their homes is a collective family unit that overflows into each other's lives, as well as the lives of extended family and friends, on a daily basis.

Visiting plays an enormous role in Arab society. People go to each other's houses routinely, with or without an invitation, as a form of entertainment as well as a means of staying connected. A carryover from the former tribal social system, hosting guests is a way of promoting family interests and staying in touch for mutual support and edification in a collective framework.

Do not expect to maintain a rigid work itinerary or a highly individualized personal schedule. Realistically, you will find yourself greeting visitors and guests frequently during work hours and at home. They look forward to your welcome and generous hospitality, which they will happily reciprocate.

While you can plan a weekend getaway or a few hours alone each day during the afternoon siesta, the rest of your day may be open to the interested, affectionate visits of business associates and personal friends.

Wasta

Wasta is an Arabic term meaning influence or clout. With enough *wasta* anything can be done. A person with *wasta* is called *Waseet* (intermediary or middleman).[6] A friend or person of influence in the right place with inside knowledge can open doors and show you shortcuts that would otherwise spell hours of extra work and roadblocks that might be insurmountable. The favor is then expected to be reciprocated. For example, an intermediary could represent your employees, if you are a manager, as someone who knows you well enough to speak on their behalf in a clear manner.

If a conflict should occur, someone with *wasta* can step in to help diffuse tensions and get things moving in a positive direction. To select the best person as the intermediary, get the advice of employees who are in a higher position than the one with whom you are in conflict. Using the services of a *waseet* shows that you are doing everything possible to make the situation right for all concerned.

Foreign companies operating in the peninsula frequently employ the services of a person who has connections to government offices and can facilitate the processing of permits. This will help to improve the workflow; without such assistance, a foreign businessperson might never get the necessary approvals from the government. A mediator of good character and a pleasant personality is worth his weight in gold.

Wasta is often called by the nickname "vitamin W." This nickname shows how *wasta* gives the user power.

Take care not to ask too much of people or overuse their willingness to help you or you may cause them to lose face. *Wasta* should only be used to open doors and to speed things up.

Humor

Humor is not only a stress reliever; it is a way to adapt to adjustments and disappointments that are an inevitable part of cross-cultural encounters. If you have visited another country previously, looking back, are you aware of faux pas that you made? Although you might have been embarrassed or cross at the time, in retrospect, you probably can laugh it off. A humorous outlook is a valuable asset to take along on all your travels.

In the Arab world, humor must be explored delicately. Comical expressions in English do not always translate well into Arabic. Cynical humor, especially at someone else's expense, should be avoided. Arabs do not like to find themselves the butt of jokes. Nor do they find amusing casual or caustic references to family members or other groups. Self-denigrating comedy is too close to Arab self-esteem for comfort, as well as a seeming rejection of their custom of honoring guests. You can't honor someone who keeps putting himself down!

However, situational humor of a gentle kind is appreciated and will find a ready audience. It is best to present a mild demeanor and a low laugh, rather than wild gesticulations and a loud guffaw, which is in keeping with the cultural tendency toward humility and conservative values.

Chapter 7

Conclusion

A Unique Opportunity

The Arabian Peninsula holds a secure place in global business. If you haven't already been engaged in professional or business matters with Arab nations, chances are you one day will. Although it is important to understand the history and traditions of the Arabian Peninsula, it is also wise to note that things are changing rapidly there, just as they are in other parts of the world.

The gradual transition from tribal rule to modern democracy is a painstaking process that continues to shape Arab society. Government hierarchy and business protocol are evolving at an unprecedented rate that demands Western corporations keep up if they want to do business in the Arabian Peninsula. Collectivism is still a dominant value, yet succeeding generations are making more individual decisions regarding marriage and careers. Women, publicly veiled, now work outside the home and manage families, just as women do in the West. Their role in society is rapidly changing and drawing curiosity, criticism, and optimism.

Western perceptions of Islam, the main religion and social code of the Arabian Peninsula, are changing as well, in the wake of events like 9-11 and increased interchanges between Western and Arab nations. These changes will continue to impact the way business is conducted in the future.

Technology also influences the way and means of doing business in the countries of the Arabian Peninsula. Personal and business computers, the Internet, and telecommunications now bridge thousands of miles in seconds to bring East and West closer than ever before.

With much to learn from each other and prospects of building cooperative business ventures that will meet important needs, the future holds exciting promise for those who seize the opportunity of doing business on the Arabian Peninsula.

Conclusion

Doing business on the Arabian Peninsula offers tremendous potential for lucrative and lasting partnerships that can bring success to everyone involved. You might even become involved with projects that help to build up the region or stabilize the Middle East, as well as enhance relations with the U.S. or promote healthy intercultural business practices. Whether you are a boss, trainee, manager, or associate, you can learn much from observing as well as engaging in commercial ventures situated on the peninsula.

Relational business negotiations begin with your first introduction to an Arab host. Your attitude will speak volumes, even when you remain verbally silent at first. Then, the manner in which you offer and return greetings, combined with your interaction with Arab customs and practices, will determine in great measure the outcome of your business projects.

As discussed in this book, your role as host or guest within a hospitality framework introduces the potential for success. First impressions are lasting, and nowhere more so than on the Arabian Peninsula where numerous factors like the following are evaluated to render a character assessment of you as a possible business partner:

- Facial expression
- Non-verbal communication
- Tone of voice
- Linguistic eloquence
- How you sit
- Hand and body gestures
- What you wear
- Who you're with
- What you say
- When you arrive
- How you respond to delays and interruptions

All of these things can speak volumes about the kind of person you are and your ability to relate to and show respect for Arab culture and customs.

In addition, your knowledge of regional and global issues that impact Arab business will be inferred from what you do and do not say, along with your attitude toward deeply-held values in the region on topics such as:

- Israel-Palestine conflict
- Terrorism-sponsoring organizations and states
- U.S. expectations of Arab nations toward terrorism
- Women's roles and rights
- Attitude toward family and elders
- Respect for status and hierarchy
- Ability to negotiate (haggle)
- Peninsula development and infrastructure
- Technology and the Internet
- Islam and morality

Your views on these and other topics are likely to influence your Arab hosts toward or away from doing business with you. Deal making in the peninsula relies as much on character as it does on capability.

This does not imply that Arabs expect Western visitors to completely assimilate or adopt an Arab mindset. Rather, the hope is that Westerners will be able to somewhat understand and accept the Arab way of doing business, no matter how alien it may seem. Of course, Arabs have a good grasp of American and European modes of conducting professional business. They are quite familiar with the conventions of the industries in which they do a large quantity of business. But like us, Arabs hope for give and take in the negotiation phase of establishing ventures and forming partnerships. Successful traders for many centuries, they bring experience and insight to the negotiating table.

While your Arab host will not expect you to share his perspective on global issues, he will trust that you keep an open mind and will make the effort to understand his view of the issues. Likewise, although you may fervently disagree with the concept of multiple wives or bringing family into the business, that is how things are done, and a good guest will not criticize his host.

Attempting to flaunt social conventions by asserting your freedoms as a democratic world citizen may invite tolerance, but will cost you respect, which in the end is often the deal breaker for intercultural negotiations in the Arab world. Bringing your wife to an all-male business meeting may result in embarrassment for all and a lost deal to boot. Making obvious your consumption of alcohol or a loose moral code could also impair business dealings. It's not that Arabs will completely reject you for questionable conduct, but they will question any public demonstration of it. Cultural sensitivity goes a long way in bridging unforeseen gaps and unplanned missteps.

Navigating the social maze will bring you to the larger context of professional conduct. In addition to the factors on which your appearance will be judged that are mentioned at the beginning of this section, your business acumen will be assessed on factors like these:

1. Poise
2. Self-confidence
3. Competent agent
4. Ability to haggle
5. Patience
6. Use of qualified interpreter and translator
7. Preparation of documents in Arabic and your native language
8. Pre-planned creative financing options
9. Adaptation to Arab business conventions
10. Trustworthy character

Lifestyle adjustments can be challenging at first to someone who is unused to the Arabian Peninsula climate and terrain. The summer days are very hot, which can take some getting used to, especially if you live in a part of the world that is typically cooler. In contrast to the heat where one might desire to wear cool summer clothing, modest dress is expected, and in fact legally mandated, for both men and women.

In particular, it can be a strain for Western married couples to avoid showing affection in public and to attend many functions separately, with husbands at all-male activities and the wives with other females. Although house pets such as cats and dogs often become part of the family in other countries, in the peninsula countries, felines and canines typically run wild, often in packs, so you won't see many domesticated varieties. However, you can bring your own pet to the region if you take appropriate precautions.

The Arabian Peninsula uses both the Gregorian calendar and the Islamic calendar—the latter is used to calculate Islamic holidays. Some Westerners find it difficult to figure out timelines on the Islamic calendar, but many locals are happy to assist.

It is important to understand that the Islamic Shar'ia law governs behavior in the region, which combines rather than separates "church and state," or in this area, "mosque and state." Moral offenses like drinking alcohol, trafficking in pornography, or using illicit drugs are punished severely. Generally, however, the crime rate remains low due to a higher standard of living derived from oil revenues, a strict Islamic code of conduct, and the traditional patriarchal system within which many families are related by blood or marriage. For the most part, Westerners are as safe or safer here as in their home countries, as long as they obey the laws.

Overall, few places in the world are as promising, exciting, and fulfilling as the Arabian Peninsula when it comes to visiting or doing business. This book highlights some areas where you may face challenges while doing business in the Arabian Peninsula. The cross-cultural understanding you gain will be a valuable tool for successfully doing business in the region. With adequate preparations and thoughtful consideration, your visit should be pleasant and rewarding for everyone involved. Doing business in Arabian Peninsula countries offers unlimited potential to explore new lands and meet interesting people while accomplishing professional and personal goals.

Appendix A: Country Differences

Bahrain

Business Hours
- Offices and shops: 7 a.m. to 2 p.m., 4 p.m. to 8 p.m., Saturday to Wednesday
- Banks: 7:30 a.m. to noon, Saturday to Wednesday; 7:30 to 11 a.m., Thursday
- Shopping centers: 9 a.m. to 9 p.m., Saturday to Thursday; 10 a.m. to 9 p.m. Friday

Business Practices
- Expect loose agendas at meetings.
- Earn your Bahrain associates' respect and trust.
- Participate in social functions as a way to build relationships.

Visas
- Available at the Bahrain International Airport or at the Saudi Arabian border
- Valid for two months, with possible extensions
- U.S. and Canada residents can purchase five-year multiple entry visas at Bahraini embassy or consulate

Ownership Laws[1]
- Non-Bahrainis can own built properties and land in designated areas.
- They can own apartments in certain categories of residential towers anywhere in Bahrain.
- They can occupy property on a leasehold basis.

Business Customs & Etiquette
- Maintain a humble and respectful attitude.

- Be considerate of local customs.
- Take a gift of flowers or chocolates if you are invited to dine with local families.

Other
- Careless (some say ruthless) taxi drivers.
- Nightlife at some of the hotels can be questionable.
- High pedestrian fatality rate.
- Alcoholic beverages are legal for non-Muslims.

Kuwait

Business Hours
- Private Offices: open at 8 a.m. Some will work until 5 p.m. and some will close at 12 p.m. and open again 4:30 to 8:30 p.m., Saturday to Thursday
- Government Offices: 8 a.m. to 2 p. m. Sunday to Thursday
- Banks: 8 a.m. to 2 p.m., Sunday to Thursday. Some branches remain open until 7 p.m. and all close at 12 p.m. on Thursday
- Post offices: 8 a.m. to noon, Sunday to Thursday
- Shopping centers: 10:30 a.m. to 12 a.m. Everyday Shops: 10:30 a.m. to 10:30 p.m., Saturday to Thursday and 4 p.m. to 10:30 p.m. On Fridays some shops will close 12:00 p.m. to 4 p. m.

Business Practices
- Combines modern with traditional business attitudes and practices.
- May be careless with time and appointments, but expect you to be on time.
- Engages in extensive international business negotiations.

Visas
- Visas are available at the airport.
- Multiple-entry visas up to 10 years are available for business on regular basis and have Kuwaiti sponsorship.

Ownership Laws
- Foreign entities can wholly own a Kuwaiti company or branch office in Kuwait.
- They might be eligible for exemptions, such as land allocation for investment purposes.
- Foreign companies and persons can lease real estate.

Business Customs & Etiquette
- Accept invitations to socialize, which are a great way to get to know Kuwaitis and be known by them.
- Do not rush into business negotiations or push for a hasty decision.
- Follow your Kuwaiti host's lead at social events.

Other
- Many areas of the desert are off-limits due to the presence of American military forces. Check with locals before going sightseeing in the desert.
- Smoking is well-tolerated here; makes for dense atmosphere in public places.
- If you are looking for an import agent or a commission agent in Kuwait, I recommend Kuwait Production Corp. E-mail: murjan71@yahoo.com.

Oman

Business Hours
- Government departments and ministries: 7:30 a.m. to 2:30 p.m., Saturday to Wednesday; 8 a.m. to 11 a.m., Thursday
- Banks: 8 a.m. to noon, Saturday to Wednesday; 8 a.m. to 11 a.m., Thursday
- Post offices: 8 a.m. to 1:30 p.m., Saturday to Wednesday; 8 a.m. to 11 a.m., Thursday
- Restaurants: 11:30 a.m. to 1:30 p.m., 5 p.m. to midnight, Saturday to Thursday; 5 p.m. to midnight, Friday
- Shops: 8 a.m. to 1 p.m., 4 p.m. to 7 or 7:30 p.m., Saturday to Wednesday; 8 a.m. to 7 p.m., Thursday

Business Practices

- Few casual or short-term jobs for tourists or students.
- Salaries tend to be low in comparison with other regions in the peninsula.

Visas

- A two-week visa is available at Seeb International Airport in Muscat for OR6.
- Obtain regular visa in advance at an Omani embassy.
- Multiple entry visas available for two years (maximum 6-month stay).
- Work visa requires sponsorship by an Omani company before entering the company.
- Overstaying a visa will result in significant charges.

Ownership Laws

- Non-Omanis can own land for residential or investment purposes in integrated tourist complexes.
- When purchasing a plot of land, you must complete the development of it within four years of land registration.
- Non-Omanis also can occupy property on a leasehold basis.

Business Customs & Etiquette

- A majority of Omanis practice an austere form of Islam but are very tolerant to others' beliefs.
- Multiculturalism contributes to a diversified society and working environment.

Other

- Hazards are flash floods and the isolation of many off-road destinations.
- Show respect visiting villages – ask permission; park beyond dwellings and paths.

Qatar

Business Hours
- Offices: 7:30 a.m. to noon, 3:30 p.m. to 7:30 p.m., Saturday to Thursday; 4 p.m. to 9 p.m., Friday
- Banks: 7:30 a.m. to 11:30 a.m., Saturday to Thursday
- Government departments: 6 a.m. to 2 p.m., Sunday to Thursday
- Post offices: 7 a.m. to 1 p.m., 4 p.m. to 7 p.m., Saturday to Thursday; 8 a.m. to 10 a.m., Friday
- Restaurants: 11:30 a.m. to 1:30 p.m., 5:30 p.m. to 11:30 p.m., Saturday to Thursday; 5 p.m. to 11:30 p.m., Friday
- Shopping centers: 10 a.m.to 10 p.m. Every day

Business Practices
- Hosted World Trade Organization Conference in 2001.
- Has developed a strong commercial infrastructure.
- It is one of the fastest-growing economies in the world.

Visas
- 30+ countries can pay QR55 for a single-entry tourist visa at Qatar's airport (complete application card on the counter in advance to save time); extensions possible.
- Apply for a multi-entry or business visa at a Qatari embassy or consulate with 3 passport photos and application in triplicate.
- Business visa applicants need a letter from the host company; visas issued within 24 hours.

Ownership Laws
- Non-Qataris may own real estate in specified areas via Ministerial Decision issued February 2006.
- Conditions of this type of ownership have not yet been published.
- Non-Qataris can occupy property on a leasehold basis and acquire long-term lease rights in certain areas.

Business Customs & Etiquette:
- Women are treated better here than in other parts of region, but still expect stares.

- Social welfare programs are advancing.
- Alcohol is available in some top-level hotel bars.

Other
- Be careful in desert areas to stay on the road and avoid soft sand and *sabkha* around coast and interior.
- Take water, tow rope, jack, and spare tire for emergency.
- There are few accommodations for disabled travelers.

Saudi Arabia

Business Hours
- Offices: 8 a.m. to 2 p.m., 4 p.m. to 7 p.m., Saturday to Wednesday; 8 a.m. to 2 p.m., Thursday
- Banks and shops: 8 a.m. to 2 p.m., 4 p.m. to 7 p.m., Saturday to Thursday
- Post offices: 7:30 a.m. to 9:30 p.m., Saturday to Wednesday
- Restaurants: 7 a.m. to 10 a.m., noon to 3 p.m., 6 p.m. to 1 p.m. Every day
- Shopping centers: 8 a.m. to 2 p.m., 4 p.m. to 11 p.m., Saturday to Thursday

Business Practices
- Frequent references to God and belief in His timing vs. man-made goals and schedules.
- Foreigners must build a relationship with Saudi associates through conservative behavior.
- Collective society and family solidarity relies on nepotism and advancement by preferment in Saudi business and government.
- Transit permission required to move about the country.
- Prepare documents in Arabic as well as in your native language.

Visas
- Must have Saudi sponsor (individual or company).
- Sponsor applies to Saudi Chamber of Commerce and Industry for approval.

- With approval, an invitation is sent to you or to embassy.
- Apply for visa in country of nationality or permanent residence.
- Present letter from your company and local chamber of commerce for visa.

Ownership Laws
- Non-Saudi investors with an investment license may possess property required for the performance of their licensed activities.
- Investment license granted to non-Saudi investor includes purchase of a building or land for the construction of buildings thereon and the investment either through a sale or lease.
- The actual cost of the project must not be less than SR30million ($8 million).
- Such investments must be realized within five years of possessing the land.
- Real estate ownership is strictly forbidden to non-Saudis in Makkah and Madinah.
- Non-Saudi nationals have the right to occupy property on a leasehold basis.

Business Customs & Etiquette
- If you try to bring in or accept forbidden things like alcohol, drugs, pork, pornography, or politically delicate material, these will be confiscated and a harsh punishments given.
- Dress conservatively – no shorts in public except on private beaches by hotels.
- Women must be covered (veiled); Western women must dress very conservatively in public.
- Women may not drive or go anywhere escorted by a man she is not related to.

UAE

Business Hours
- Banks: 8 a.m. to 2 p.m. or 4 p.m. Saturday to Wednesday; 8 a.m. to noon, Thursday

- Government offices: 8 a.m. to 2 p.m., Saturday to Wednesday; Thursday mornings – try to go before 1 p.m.
- Private offices: 8 or 9 a.m. to 5 or 6 p.m. Saturday to Wednesday; some close on Saturday. Some will close in the afternoon for 4 hours, then open again until 8 or 9 p.m.
- Shopping malls: 10 a.m. to 12 a.m. Every day (Closed for Friday prayers 11:30 a.m. to 1:30 p.m.)
- Shops and *souqs*: 9 a.m. to 1 p.m., 4 p.m. to 9 p.m., Saturday to Thursday, 4 p.m. to 9 p.m., Friday

Business Practices
- Expect to conduct business over numerous cups of Arabic coffee.
- Businessmen have a shrewd, cosmopolitan approach to global business.
- Women's roles are gradually changing; many are taking jobs outside the home.
- Internet access is widely available, along with postal services and fax machines.

Visas
- 30-day visits available at approved airports, and land & seaports for Dh100.
- Extensions available.
- Many hotels can arrange visas when you book with them ahead of time.

Ownership Laws
- Abu Dhabi: Non-UAE nationals have the right to own buildings on a plot of land in an investment zone but not the land itself.
- Non-UAE nationals also may enjoy Usufruct and Musataha (development) rights in relation to allocated plots of land, buildings, and installations.
- Non-UAE nationals have the right to occupy properties on a leasehold basis.
- Dubai: non-UAE nationals will be permitted to own properties in certain parts of Dubai on a freehold basis.

Business Customs & Etiquette
- Expect a combination of traditional and modern customs.
- Do not ask after an Arab's wife or other female relatives, nor gaze at females directly.
- Several business meetings may take place before a decision is made.
- Expect and offer negative information, including rejections, to be given gently and indirectly.

Other
- Dangerous speeding & careless drivers.
- Rip tides at swimming beaches.
- Expatriate population is 80%.

Yemen

Business Hours
- Closed during afternoon *qat* (*kot*) chewing 1 p.m. to 6 p.m.
- Banks: 8 a.m. to noon, Saturday to Thursday; open to 11 a.m., Thursday
- Government offices: 8 a.m. to 3 p.m. Saturday to Wednesday; many close by 1 or 1:30 p.m.
- Post offices: 8:30 a.m. to 1 p.m., 3:30 p.m. to 7 p.m., Saturday to Thursday; often open from 7 p.m. to 8 p.m., Friday
- Restaurants: 7 a.m. to 9 p.m.; times changeable in larger towns
- Shops and private businesses: 9 a.m. to noon, 4 p.m. to 8 p.m., Saturday to Thursday; some Friday hours
- Telecom and internet centers: 7 a.m. to 10 p.m. Daily.

Business Practices
- Oil represents 70% of the country's revenue, agriculture, 20%.
- 45% of the people live below the U.N. poverty rate of $2 per day.
- Companies struggle to find qualified employees and often hire immigrants.
- Many women work and drive.

Visas

- Visa requirements change frequently – check with embassy or consulate.
- You'll need your passport, one or two passport size photos, fee of US$50 to US$100, and SASE if by mail.
- Business visa needs special application and letter of introduction from company or college.
- Get visa at San'a airport up to one month for U.S. citizens and EU citizens up to three months.
- Israelis or travelers to Israel with stamp in passport will be denied visa to Yemen.
- Travel permit needed within Yemen.

Ownership Laws

- Foreigners may own property, but as a practical matter, should plan to engage a Yemini partner.

Business Customs & Etiquette

- Don't expect Yemeni host to open your gift in front of you, nor should you open his in his presence.
- Be aware of the afternoon custom of chewing *qat* (*kot*) after the siesta; you may be asked to join.
- Keep local tourist police informed of changes in your itinerary and transit visa.

Other

- Watch for *qat* chewers, animals, and children on the roads.
- Check road conditions in outlying areas before setting out; there are few signs and flooding causes considerable damage.
- Low crime rate.
- Huge potential for increased tourism.
- Be wary of unrecovered land mines at old North/South Yemen borders.
- Avoid Mideast political discussions.

Appendix B: Dos and Don'ts in the Arabian Peninsula

Issue:	Do:	Don't:
Oral Communication	• Exchange pleasantries before conducting business • Arab communication is high-context • Become familiar with *"musayra"* • Use a gracious tone • Use face-saving strategies to protect Arab associates' honor	• Don't excessively admire someone's possession or he'll have to give it to you • Don't display a loud public voice or obvious anger • Don't embarrass Arab host, friends, associates • Don't be too direct
Nonverbal Communication	• Show humility • Be respectful • Use right hand for food, smoking, passing things • Learn meaning of gestures	• Don't use left hand to greet or eat with • Don't show sole of foot • Don't let silence bother you
Written Communication	• Prepare documents in Arabic and English • Use a reliable translator	• Don't translate English verbatim as it could be confusing or misunderstood • Don't keep careless records
Friendships and Relationships	• Build social relationships while conducting business	• Don't leave too early or too late when visiting

	• Earn trust with credible reputation • Leave wife at home unless she's specifically invited	• Don't ask about an Arab's wife or female relative or show interest in a female • Don't escort unrelated females in public
Meetings and Appointments	• Plan to arrive on time • Expect meeting interruptions • Expect long but few sessions	• Don't necessarily expect Arab associates to be timely • Don't impose a firm agenda
Etiquette	• Use correct hand gestures • Adapt to hierarchical order • Drink at least one cup of tea or coffee when visiting • Dress conservatively in public • Wear a suit for business meetings	• Don't point with finger • Don't open gifts in front of giver, or expect Arabs to • Don't offer alcohol or pork to Muslims • Don't call during siesta or prayer times
Contracts	• Prepare English and Arabic copies • Be sure they are detailed and clear	• Don't let contract substitute for positive business relationship • Follow correct procedures, which may vary from your home country
Negotiating	• Hire an agent to coordinate negotiations • Expect Arab first offers to buy low and sell high, with room to negotiate	• Don't accept first offer unless it meets your goals • Don't offer a price that is too close to bottom line; re-

	• Become familiar with the *Suq* method • Try to use an intermediary with *wasta*	serve negotiating room • Don't cause your counterpart to lose face
Telephone and Internet	• Cell phones are called "mobiles" • Telephone offices and Internet cafes are widely available for general use	• Don't forget to check mobile phone equipment needs before departure • Don't expect your laptop to be usable without an adapter
Beliefs and Values	• Arabs are family-centered • Honor and hospitality are always offered to guests • Arab culture is polychronic • Islamic faith permeates outlook and daily life	• Don't try to talk business immediately or all the time • Don't neglect to establish a social relationship or friendship as business foundation • Don't use cutthroat tactics

Appendix C: Arab Business Proverbs

Arabs make abundant use of proverbs. A person's knowledge of proverbs demonstrates their wisdom and insight.

The successful international manager will seek information about the Arab culture from all sources, including proverbs. The following proverbs are some of the more common used in business. They illuminate the Arab outlook on life and business and will provide you insight into the culture. You can also impress your Arab host with your knowledge of them.

(Meanings are given in italics when not obvious.)

Only a fool tests the depth of water with both feet.
If you have much, give of your wealth; if you have little, give of your heart.
Save your bright penny for a dark day.
Ask the experienced, not the learned.
A known mistake is better than an unknown truth.
The world is changeable, one day honey and the next day onions.
Every sun has to set.
The dogs may bark but the caravan moves on. *(A person should rise above petty criticism.)*
Patience is beautiful.
Show your enemy your sword and your gold.
Be careful of the one who smiles in front of you with a white tooth, inside him is a black heart.
The ass that goes to Mecca remains an ass. *(A place or forum does not make you or your words better.)*
Beware the man who you have only seen smile. *(Looks can be deceiving.)*
Exert effort; you shall be rewarded.
If you conduct yourself properly, fear no one.

A man with one plan goes out to execute it; a man with two plans becomes perplexed.

A promise is a cloud; fulfillment is rain.

Examine what is said, not him who speaks.

Example is better than precept.

He who has health has hope; and he who has hope, has everything.

It is good to know the truth, but it is better to speak of palm trees. *(You should not say everything you know.)*

Live together like brothers and do business like strangers.

Write bad things that are done to you in sand, but write the good things that happen to you on a piece of marble.

When you shoot an arrow of truth, dip its point in honey.

Beware: some liars tell the truth.

Lie to a liar, for lies are his coin; Steal from a thief, for that is easy; lay a trap for a trickster and catch him at first attempt, but beware of an honest man.

We learn little from our successes, but a lot from our failures.

Make your bargain before beginning to plow.

Do not buy a fish in the water.

No answer is an answer.

Sit crooked and speak straight.

The best talk is short and to the point.

Let the baker bake your bread even if he eats half of it. (*It is better to assign work to specialists.*)

Debt is worry at night and humiliation during the day.

A promise is an obligation.

What is in the heart will be uncovered by the tongue.

He who does not lose does not gain.

Judge a person by his ethics, not by what he wears.

Humiliate your money not yourself. *(Don't humiliate yourself for the sake of money.)*

The one who slanders others in front of you will slander you in front of others.

If I listen, I have the advantage; if I speak, others have it.

Appendix D: Arabic Business Terms

Plurals are shown in brackets

English	**Transliteration**
advisor	mudyshsaar (mustashaareen)
agent	alwakel
Arab Gulf	Al-Khaleej Al-Arabee
assistant	muaawin (muaawineen)
bank	baank
certificate	shahaada
clock/hour/watch	saa'a (saa'aat)*
commerce/trade	tijaara
complaint	shakwa
contract	aqd (uqood)
cost	qeema
customs (airport)	jumruk
date	taareekh
day	yome (ayaam)
difference between	farq bane
difficult	saa'b
director	mudeer (mudara)
dollar	doolar (doolaaraat)
employee	mwadhdhaf (muwadhdhafeen)
engineer	muhandis (muhandiseen)
envelope	dharf (dhuroof)
equipment	jihaaz (ajhiza)
exhibition	ma'rid
expense	masroof (massaareef)
expensive	ghaalee
expert (in)	khabeer (bi)
exporter	almosader
exports	saadiraat
finally	akheeran

free	hurr
gasoline (petrol)	benzene
gift	hadeeya (hadaayaa)
gulf	khaleej
hire	eejaar
hotel	funduq
how?	kayf?
how many/how much?	kam?
immediately	haalan
he imported	istawrad
he imports	yastawrid
importer	almostwrd
imports	waaridaat
important	muhim
information	khabar
international	duwalee
invitation	da'wa
job	wadheefa
law	qaanoon (qawaaneen)
leader	qaa'id (quwaad)
letter	maktoob
machine	makeena
manager	mudeer (mudaraa)
market	suq
meeting	ijtimaa' (ijtimaa'aat)
merchant	taajir (tujjaar)
message	risaala (rasaa'il
Middle East	Ash-Sharq AlOwsat
million	milyoon (malaayeen)
Ministry of Commerce	Wizaaret At-Tijaara
minute	daqeeqa (daqaa'iq)
mistake	ghalat
modern	hadeeth
money	fuloos
Mr.	saiyid
name	ism (asmaa)
no	la
number	raqm (arqaam)

office	maktab (makaatib)
oil (petroleum)	naft
on the subject of ...	bikhusoos
only	fuqut/bass
opportunity	fursa
or	aw
paper (pieces of)	woroqa (awraaq)
part (of)	juz (ajzaa)
passport	jawaaz safar
pen	qolum hibr
permission/permit	rukhsa
place	mahal
possible	mumkin
post	bareed
Post Office	Maktab Al-Bareed
present (adj.)	haalee
present (gift)	hadeeya (hadaayaa)
principal (main)	raeesee
problem	mushkila (mashaakil)
prohibited	mamnoo'
question	su'aal (as'ila)
rent	eejaar
report	taqreer (taqaareer)
reservation	hajz
responsible(for)	mas'ool
responsibility	mas'ooleeya
result (of)	nateeja
service	khidma
at your service	fee khidmatak
shop	dukkaan (dakaakeen)
specialist	ikhsaa'ee
tax	dareeba (daraa-ib)
technical (adj)	fannee
telephone	telefoon
	(*cell phone* = "mobiiel")
thousand	elf (aalaaf)
tomorrow	bukra
tourism	seeyaaha

until	hatta
valid	jayyid
value	qeema
weight	wazn
whole	kul
with	ma
without	bidoon
wireless	la silkee
work	shogl or amal
writing paper	woroq al-kitaaba
wrong (adj.)	ghaltaan
yes	aiwa or na'am
	(*yeah* = "ee")
yesterday	ams
zero	sifar

* *The Arabic letter* ayn *has no English equivalent. It is similar to the glottal stop (sounds like the closing of the throat before saying 'oh-oh') and is represented here by an apostrophe (').*

Add Your Own Words Here

Appendix E: Useful Web Sites

Accommodations
http://www.cyberrentals.com/middle-east/s/773/fa/find.squery
http://www.sublet.com/Region_Rentals/MiddleEast_Rentals.asp
http://www.vast.com/vacation_rentals/region-Middle-East

Computer Remote Access
http://www.gotomypc.com
http://pcnow.webex.com

Connecting with the Arab Market
U.S. Department of Commerce's International Trade Administration provides trade leads, market research, counseling, and more information from 19 government agencies to help you navigate the export process to the Middle East at http://www.export.gov. Choose the link titled "Find Country Information" Then "Middle East and North Africa Business Information Center."

The Department of Commerce also maintains up-to-date information on laws, taxes, and regulations and publishes market research reports for each country: http://www.buyusa.gov

For trade leads and market research, see the National Trade Data Bank: http://www.stat-usa.gov/tradtest.nsf

Find exporters and importers at Trade Key: http://www.tradekey.com/

For customs updates, shipping information, news, and much more go to The Journal of Commerce Web site: http://www.joc.com/

International Import-Export Trade Leads is a directory that will help you find international partners: http://www.tradeleadscenter.com/

This Web site lists trade leads from all over the world (registration required): http://b2b.tradeholding.com/

Country Profiles
http://www.state.gov/r/pa/ei/bgn
http://www.al-bab.com/

Currency Converter
http://www.xe.com

Discount Airfares
http://www.economytravel.com/

Documentary Requirements for Exports to the Peninsula
Arab countries require that commercial invoices be certified either by the National U.S.-Arab Chamber of Commerce (tel: 202-289-5920) or, in the case of the United Arab Emirates, by the Arab American Chamber of Commerce and legalized by each respective country's consulate.

US-Arab Chamber of Commerce Web site: http://www.nusacc.org/
Arab American Chamber of Commerce Web site: http://www.arabchamber.org/uae/index.htm

Ease of Doing Business
The World Bank Group – Doing Business Project. This site provides objective measures of business regulations and enforcement. Just go to the home page below and type in the desired country to get the overall "ease of doing business" ranking and see how the country ranks in ten select business topics. http://www.doingbusiness.org/

Holidays
Business holidays can be found on the International Business Center Web site at
http://www.internationalbusinesscenter.com/international_calendar.html

Internet Phones
http://www.skype.com
http://www.vonage.com

Market Intelligence
Middle East Economic Digest (MEED)
http://www.meed.com/index.html
Business Intelligence – Middle East: News and business intelligence by country and sector. Site allows you to create your own custom homepage. http://www.bi-me.com/

Ernst & Young
http://www.ey.com/global/Content.nsf/Middle_East/Home_-_Test

Plug Adapters

For travel accessories, voltage guide, and plug guide see
http://www.travel-accessories-products.com/voltage_guide.htm

Telephones

For an international pay-as-you go phone with no contract try the Mobal phone. http://www.mobal.com

To see if your phone will work in the country you are traveling to and for explanation of the different "bands" go to:
http://www.thetravelinsider.info/roadwarriorcontent/quadbandphones.htm

Voltage, outlets, international phones, dialing codes

http://www.kropla.com

Notes

Chapter 1

1. U.S. Census Bureau, Foreign Trade Statistics Web site. www.census.gov/foreign-trade/balance/index.html "US Trade in Goods by Country" (accessed January 28, 2008)
2. Islamic law.
3. B. Ingham, *Customs & Eetiquette of Arabia and the Gulf States* (Kent, England: Global Books Limited, 1994), 12-13.
4. L.A. Samovar, and R.E. Porter, eds. *Intercultural Communication: A Reader*. 10th ed. (Belmont, CA: Wadsworth, 2003), 244.
5. J. Al-Omari, *The Arab Way: How to Work More Effectively with Arab Cultures* (Oxford, U.K.: How To Books, 2003), 31.
6. D. W. Hendon, R.A. Hendon, and P. Herbig, *Cross-cultural Business Negotiations* (Westport, CT: Praeger, 1999), 165.

Chapter 2

1. Al-Omari, *The Arab Way*, 33.
2. Al-Omari, *The Arab Way*, 38.
3. Samovar and Porter, *Intercultural Communication*, 262.
4. Samovar and Porter, *Intercultural Communication*, 242.
5. Samovar and Porter, *Intercultural Communication*, 226-228.
6. Israeli-Jews on the other hand use a speech code called *dugri* which is direct, pragmatic, argumentative, and assertive; it is the opposite of Arab *musayra* speech code, thus the difficulty with dialogue and negotiation between the two groups.
7. M. K. Nydell, *Understanding Arabs: A Guide for Westerners*. 3rd ed. (Yarmouth, Maine: Intercultural Press, 2002), 115.
8. International Herald Tribune, "Foreign Language Courses Booming on US College Campuses" November 13, 2007.
9. M. D. Al-Sabt, *Arabian Business and Cultural Guide: Your Guide to Do's and Don'ts in the Arabian Culture & Market*. (TradersCity.com, 2006), 20.

10. Al-Sabt, *Arabian Business*, 19.
11. J. Williams, *Don't They Know it's Friday?* (Dubai, UAE: Motivate Publishing, 1998), 57.
12. Hendon, Hendon, and Herbig, *Cross-cultural Business Negotiations*, 68-69.
13. This example also shows the confusion that can occur with intercultural communication between people from two high-context cultures. Both of the men in the story were from different, high-context cultures and missed the subtle hints from the other.
14. D. A. Victor, "Doing Business in the Arab World." In *Encyclopedia of Business, 2nd ed. - A-Ar,* ed. J. Malonis. Thomson Gale. http://www.referenceforbusiness.com/encyclopedia/A-Ar/Arab-World-Doing-Business-in-the.html#LANGUAGE (accessed October 31, 2007).
15. Williams, *Don't They Know it's Friday?,* 43.
16. Williams, *Don't They Know it's Friday?,* 45.

Chapter 3
1. Hendon, Hendon, and Herbig *Cross-cultural Business Negotiations*, 176-178.
2. J. L. Esposito, *What Everyone Needs to Know About Islam.* (Oxford, NY: Oxford University, 2002), 167-168.
3. K. C. Shippey, *A Short Course in International Contracts: Drafting the International Sales Contract for Attorneys and Non-attorneys.* 2nd ed. (San Rafael, CA: World Trade Press, 2002), 29.

Chapter 4
1. J. B. Cullen, and K. Parboteeah, *Multinational Management: A Strategic Approach* 4th ed. (Mason, OH: Thomson, 2008), 653-669.
2. Cullen and Parboteeah, *Multinational Management,* 661.
3. Cullen and Parboteeah, *Multinational Management,* 662.
4. J.E. Curry, *A Short Course in International Negotiating: Planning and Conducting International Commercial Negotiations.* (San Rafael, CA: World Trade Press., 1999), 164.
5. Adapted from Curry, *A Short Course in International Negotiating.*

6.   Curry, *A Short Course in International Negotiating,* 125-129.

7.   Cullen and Parboteeah, *Multinational Management,* 670-671.

Chapter 5

1.   L. Laroche, "Doing Business in the Arab World: Etiquette and Customs." *CMA Management,* December 1, 2000, 53.

2.   Williams, *Don't They Know it's Friday?* 64.

3.   Al-Sabt, *Arabian Business and Cultural Guide,* 49-51.

4.   Al-Sabt, *Arabian Business and Cultural Guide,* 53.

5.   Al-Sabt, *Arabian Business and Cultural Guide,* 55-58.

Chapter 6

1.   F. Linzee Gordon, and A. Ham, *Arabian Peninsula* (Oakland, CA: Lonely Planet, 2004), 39.

2.   M.K. Nydell, *Understanding Arabs: A Guide for Westerners.* 3rd ed. (Yarmouth, Maine: Intercultural Press, 2002), p 58-59.

3.   Linzee Gordon and Ham, *Arabian Peninsula,* 34.

4.   Linzee Gordon and Ham, *Arabian Peninsula,* 45-46.

5.   Linzee Gordon and Ham, *Arabian Peninsula,* 448-449.

6.   The base noun for *wasta* is *wasat* which means middle, hence the Arabic term for the Middle East: *Asharq* (east) *Al-Awsat* (middle).

Chapter 7

Appendix A

1.   Ownership laws listed in Appendix A are from A.H. Mohammed, "Caveat Investor." *Gulf Property.* September 2007, 18-19.

Reference List

Al-Omari, J. 2003. *The Arab way: How to work more effectively with Arab cultures.* Oxford, U.K.: How To Books.

Al-Sabt, M. D. 2006. *Arabian business and cultural guide: Your guide to do's and don'ts in the Arabian culture & market.* TradersCity.com.

Cullen, J. B., and Parboteeah, K. P. 2008. *Multinational management: A strategic approach.* 4th ed. Mason, OH: Thomson.

Curry, J. E. 1999. *A short course in international negotiating: Planning and conducting international commercial negotiations.* San Rafael, CA: World Trade Press.

Esposito, J. L. 2002. *What everyone needs to know about Islam.* Oxford, NY: Oxford University.

Foreign Affairs and International Trade Canada. 2004. *Doing business in the Middle East.* http://www.dfait-maeci.gc.ca/middle_east/doing_business-en.asp. (accessed January 22, 2008).

Hendon, D. W., Hendon, R. A., and Herbig, P. 1999. *Cross-cultural business negotiations.* Westport, CT: Praeger.

Ingham, B. 1994. *Customs & etiquette of Arabia and the Gulf States.* Kent, UK: Global Books.

International Herald Tribune. "Foreign Language Courses Booming on US College Campuses." November 13, 2007.

Laroche, L. Doing business in the Arab world: Etiquette and customs. *CMA Management.* December 1, 2000, 53.

Linzee Gordon, F., Maxwell, V., Walker J., and Ham, A. 2004 Arabian Peninsula. 2004. Oakland, CA: Lonely Planet.

McGrane, S. J. 2005. Arab cultural and communication patterns.

Mohammed, A. H. Caveat investor. *Gulf Property.* September 2007. 18-19.

Nydell, M.K. 2002. *Understanding Arabs: A guide for westerners.* 3rd ed. Yarmouth, Maine: Intercultural Press.

Samovar, L. A., and Porter, R. E., eds. 2003. *Intercultural communication: A reader.* 10th ed. Belmont, CA: Wadsworth.

Shippey, K. C. 2002. A short course in international contracts: Drafting the international sales contract for attorneys and non-attorneys. 2nd ed. San Rafael, CA: World Trade Press.

U.S. Census Bureau, Foreign Trade Statistics. http://www.census.gov/foreign-trade/balance/index.html US Trade in Goods by Country (accessed January 28, 2008).

Victor, D. A. 2006. Doing Business in the Arab World. In *Encyclopedia of Business, 2nd ed. - A-Ar,* ed. J. Malonis. Thomson Gale. http://www.referenceforbusiness.com/encyclopedia/A-Ar/Arab-World-Doing-Business-in-the.html#LANGUAGE (accessed October 31, 2007).

Williams, J. 1998. *Don't they know it's Friday?* Dubai, UAE: Motivate Publishing.

Index

151